Tempus ORAL HISTORY *Series*

Evesham
voices

Mrs Eyres Monsell receiving a bouquet at the Old English Fete in 1909.

Tempus ORAL HISTORY *Series*

Evesham
voices

Compiled by
Genevieve Tudor and Amy Douglas

TEMPUS

First published 2000
Copyright © Genevieve Tudor and Amy Douglas, 2000

Tempus Publishing Limited
The Mill, Brimscombe Port,
Stroud, Gloucestershire, GL5 2QG

ISBN 0 7524 2092 5

Typesetting and origination by
Tempus Publishing Limited
Printed in Great Britain by
Midway Clark Printing, Wiltshire

The Almonry Museum and the stocks outside, Evesham. Many thanks to the Almonry who supplied many of the photographs for this book.

Contents

On the river.

Introduction

In December 1999 we began a reminiscence project within four sheltered accommodation housing schemes: Ferryview, Meade Court, Bewdley Court and Charles Close. Wychaven District Council and West Midland Arts commissioned the project with support from Evesham and Pershore Housing Association.

As the year 2000 dawned people realized just how much oral history could be, and has been, lost to us because we have not taken steps to record and write down the memories and stories of those who are still with us and can tell the tales of how it really was …

Evesham is a fascinating place in which to work. It also has the highest percentage of octogenarians in the country. We knew this would mean a wealth of memories about the town and its surrounding villages would be available from those we talked to. We were not disappointed. Thank you to all those who welcomed us into their homes and shared their memories and knowledge with us.

Evesham is a very special place, a meeting place of people, and a haven for the BBC during

The riverside at Evesham.

the war and the heart of English agriculture. This book is just one result of the reminiscence project and is intended to provide a resource for the people of Evesham.

We were given such a multitude of stories, history and anecdotes; it was unfortunately impossible to include everyone. This book represents only a taster of what we recorded. If it is enough to wet your appetite you will be able to find many more interesting facts and information at the Almonry Museum in the centre of the town and an extremely active and interesting Historical Society, which you may consider joining.

Our grateful thanks go to the Almonry and the Evesham Historical Society, who allowed us to include many of the photographs they have collected. Our interviewees contributed other photographs and are credited where due. We hope you enjoy reading this book as much as we enjoyed the research and the writing of it.

Genevieve Tudor and Amy Douglas

List of Contributors

Bill Atkinson, born 1921
Wilfred John Ayres, born 1916
Isabelle Beckley, born 1915
Lottie Buckingham, born 1923
Nick Capaldi, born 1913
Honor Clements, born 1915
Gladys Davis, born 1911
Sandra Grady, born 1943
Doris Greenhalf, born 1913
Doris Haines, born 1913
Barbara Harris, born 1914
Doris Hartland, born 1918
Annie Harwood, born 1905
Ethel Marion Heritage, born 1913
Sylvia Hickenbothan, born 1913
Bernard Hunt, born 1922
Florence Edna Elizabeth Hunt, born 1927
Betty Jones, born 1910
Phyllis Reay, born 1914
Harold Robinson, born 1908
Doris Saunders, born 1913
Joe Sherwood, born 1923
Dorothy May Sollis, born 1921
Kate Spilsbury, born 1911
Olive Thould, born 1918
Mrs Townley, born 1915
Catherine Maude Turner, born 1902

CHAPTER 1

Childhood and Growing Up

Ethel Marion Heritage as a baby, 1913.

Schooldays

Big School

I went to St Stevens in Worcester, it was attached to a church. I had a brother and a sister that were going and of course I wanted to go, so they let me go, though I wasn't really old enough. We had slates and slate pencils and a blackboard.

Annie Harwood, born 1905

The Welsh Anthem

I didn't mind school. When my dad was down in Wales, I went to school in Wales a bit and I could sing the Welsh anthem all the way through in Welsh and when we come up into the Midlands, the girls used to get me in the toilet and try and make me to sing this Welsh anthem. Then I went to Fladbury and I didn't go to the big school, it wasn't built, I only went to the infants, but my eldest brother, he was quite good, you know what I mean, he wasn't dull and my eldest brother, the school master at Fladbury said he didn't want him to work on the land because everybody worked on the land in those days. He went on to school for a bit and he tried to learn him the shorthand and that, but my mum and dad was poor and we hadn't got the money in them days, so Harry left and he went on the land to live. My sister passed to the grammar school twice, but mum and dad hadn't got the money to send her, you had to pay in them days.

Doris Saunders, born 1913

Putting on the Kettle

Miss Owen, I'll always remember, I was in the infants then. You had to fill a kettle, big iron kettle, in the first break, and you had to put it on a little trivet in front. Of course we had a coal fire, and put it on there and mum used to put a little bit of cocoa and a little bit of sugar in a little tiny mustard tin. We used to put it in the cup and Miss Owen, she used to put this boiling water on for our drink and that's all we had at dinner time, just a drink of cocoa and you took a bit of food. I know there was a girl, Nancy (she's dead now) and she was better off than me – we was very poor – and she always used to give me a sandwich of hers. I always think about it. When we first come to Fladbury, we lived right on the top of Fladbury hill and there was only my brother and Lil and Harry wasn't school age, and mum said 'you'd better walk down to school

Merstow Green Coronation Dinner, 1911.

Merstow Green School.

to see how long it's going to take'. We was away about three hours I think, but we had to walk across fields and down there to school and I remember black stockings and hobnailed boots, oh dear, honest, we was very poor. But we never got into any trouble and we never owed anybody anything, my dad wouldn't let you have anything without paying for it. He was very strict.

Doris Saunders, born 1913

Merstow Green School

We was boys and girls separate in those days. We were amalgamated just before I left school. We had one mistress – she was a real dragon – but she kept order. We had one school teacher. He was only young. He used to be writing at the blackboard and you'd have a chunk of chalk chucked at you. We had a teacher who had hay fever – she used to sneeze and that would tickle us kids to death. They've closed the school down now. Merstow Green, my grandfather went there. My father went there – and I went there and my son Tom went there. I was three when I went to school, used to play with sand in the tray and we used to have beads and wire. We used to thread them. We walked to school we lived just through the alley. We learnt to read and write when we were five.

Doris Greenhalf, born 1913

Hot Milk in the Teacher's Kitchen

We just leant the basic things, nothing out of the ordinary, it was just an ordinary little village school. There was the infants and then there was another set of classes and then Miss Hipkins, whose class I was in. That was all the teachers we had – three, I suppose, and they were all ladies. Every morning somebody used to go up to the farm and fetch a big can of milk and we used to go into the teacher's kitchen and hot it up and those that needed it or wanted it could have a cup of hot milk. That was given to us. I don't know who bought the milk, it was given to us. I always used to have my cup of milk, it was lovely.

Isabelle Beckley, born 1915

The Bug Rake

I went to school in Badsey. I loved school because I had someone to play with. One of the teachers was called Miss Smith, she was a pupil teacher. I don't remember much about the first class – only that I caught nits! I had to go home and have what they called the 'bug rake'. Miss Smith was in the 2nd class. She used to teach music. I always ended up with the clapper, the triangle, and I always wanted to play the cymbals but I never got that far. She used to make things. One year she made a fair out of cardboard and it all worked, the Ginny horses went round. She used pipe cleaners and lollipop sticks. The swing boats worked. I loved it, being in her class.

It was quite a big school, there were about thirty-eight or forty in a class. I used to do a lot of sport. I won fifty points once for playing cricket against the boys. I was the maiden they couldn't bowl over! Two years I came fourth in needlework, I liked that because I got a shilling.

Sandra Grady, born 1943

Cold Classrooms

By the time I got to school some of them (my brothers and sisters) had left school and were working and living elsewhere, so by the time I was at school, [getting ready for school] wasn't too overcrowded. I went to school at St Mary's in the High Street. In those days there were no school buses and it meant walking to school from Bengeworth, and no school meals, so you took sandwiches with you. In the winter, when it was really very cold, one of the teachers would make some soup and we'd have a cup of soup or something to warm us up. There was no heating in the classroom, just one fire in the middle of the room, other than that there was no heating whatever.

Wilfred Ayres, born 1916

Open Air School

I went to an open air school for twelve months. We didn't do many lessons, we just had to live in the open air all the time, it's because I had a weak chest. There used to be one at Malvern, but I used to go to the one at Worcester, so I used to go home at night. The one at Malvern they had to 'live in'. We did a lot of reading poetry and stuff like that, nothing very strenuous. We did a few little exercises and walked around the park – it was in the park. Every afternoon we had to lie down for so long and have a rest. It was in a big wooden building, more or less like a shed actually. The front of it was all open because we had to have this fresh air all the time. I lay there many a time with the rain or the snow blowing in on us. But we did have to be wrapped up well. We had to wear hand-knitted long stockings because they were very, very keen, you had to cover up your thighs – these days it sounds ridiculous when they go round with their skirts up here! – but we had to keep our thighs covered up with warm things. We only had certain things to eat. It did me good actually, because before that I was a bit faddy with my food apparently. I suppose, being the only one, my mother fussed over me a bit and if I didn't like a thing, I wasn't forced to eat it. But being there you had to and it wasn't very nice at first! I didn't like porridge. Now, I went home to sleep, but we had to be there early and have our breakfast there and every morning it was porridge with two thick pieces of bread and margarine – it wasn't butter, we always had butter at home. And I didn't like thick pieces; I liked them cut thin. But you had to eat two pieces. You could eat more, but you couldn't have less. And I remember, I sat looking at these pieces of bread and the lady, Miss Holmes, came round. And I said 'Please Miss Holmes, I don't like porridge', 'Well you'll eat it here'. And she walked around this table again, there was only sixteen of us at one long table and she dug me in the back and said, 'Get and eat that porridge!' 'But I don't like it.' 'Well you'll eat it,' and she picked up the spoon and started feeding me! I think that upset me more than anything, it hurt my dignity to have her feeding me – I think I was eight! So I had to eat the porridge and these blessed thick pieces of bread. But it did me good and I like porridge now! It was just the same thing at teatime, we had this thick bread and my Grandma came and asked if she could bring some jam for us. Well she was told she could bring some, but only if she brought enough for everybody. Well that was lovely.

Almswood School, c. 1913.

Sedgeberrow School in the early 1920s. Ethel Marion Heritage is in the top right hand corner.

There was a man lived near there and he used to grow salad things and from time to time he used to bring some of that down. Now before that I would never eat spring onions or radishes, but of course we were glad to have anything with this awful thick bread and margarine. Now I love them, I love anything like that.

Phyllis Reay, born 1914

Playtime

Playing in the Street

We'd go out into the front to play. It was a very narrow street, it still is, two cars couldn't pass each other properly. It was all cobbly, bricks. We used to go skipping, jumping, as we called it, over the rope, we used to keep highering it and highering it until you fell over and then you were out:

I am a girl guide, dressed in blue
These are the things that I must do
Put your hands on your head,
Then on your hips,
Now you go and do the flips

… and then you used to have to jump over quick at the end.

And they weren't those thin ropes, we used to have the thick ropes, if it caught your legs it really hurt! They were very thick, like a tow rope, it used to take two hands to turn them around, they were that heavy. Of course there were about seventeen or eighteen children lived in that row of houses where I lived.

Dorothy May Sollis, born 1921

Jabbing on the Brakes

We used to play skipping and in the winter when it snowed we'd make long slides down Horsebridge Road and get told off for that. It was all right for us kids but not other people. Now I tell 'them' off. Before the village hall was built at Badsey some of the boys would take their bikes and ride round and round in a circle – it was a piece of waste ground and I hadn't got a bike then, so I went and got mother's bike and I ruined the tyres jabbing the brakes on. She wasn't best pleased. It was a lovely bike, the handlebars were higher than the seat and I'd only got little legs you see.

Sandra Grady, born 1943

Scarlet Fever

Somebody lit a fire behind the back of the memorial hall at Badsey. There were three of us out the front and Mr Haines (the local policeman) came and collared us and said we'd no business lighting fires. We didn't light it but we got told off. He'd give you a clip before he told your dad, and you got another one then. He used to come along on his bike and you didn't know he was there till he was up behind you. One time we played on the sewerage thing – going round and round – I was the only one who caught scarlet fever. We used to go out for hours, but we were all right, we all stuck together.

When I was older I used to work on the land because my cousin had a bit of ground up Bowers Hill and he used to take us up in the back of his pick up. We'd sit in the back and we'd go pea picking. It was great fun that was. We'd do a bit then go off to climb the trees than go back and do some more. I wasn't much of a lady at all! Uncle used to give us money to go to the pictures for doing the work.

Sandra Grady, born 1943

Flick Ha'penny

I'll tell you another thing we used to do when we were children. My mother had a table that she scrubbed, a white table, not a posh one you polished, you didn't have them in those days, but a white table which you had to scrub. Well, we used to have what was called a football team, us children, the whole street was in the football team. Well my brothers on this table, they marked a football pitch, marked it out with a proper marker, you could never get it off – my mother had to put up with lot of things, I can tell you, then they'd come in at night, more so in the winter than the summer because we were always out in the summer, and the kids'd come in, as many as we could get in. The others had to come the next night if they couldn't get in that night and we had what we called a peg – a piece of wood, then my brothers used to shape it into a point at the end. Then we had a ha'penny and that was the ball. We had to put it on the line and then there was two of us played, you had to flick it with the peg until the first one scored a goal. One at one end and one at the other. Then out of silver paper out of the cigarettes – they used to make it into a big cup like a Challenge cup. It used to take them weeks. Then we used to play for this cup at flick ha'penny we called it. I think everybody won the cup at some time because we played for years.

Dorothy May Sollis, born 1921

Sundays and Scrumping

Up in the morning, breakfast, Sunday school, church and we were allowed out of church when the sermons started, so we used to go to church then we'd troop out when he used to go in the pulpit and then Sunday afternoon, Sunday school again and then at night my father used to sing in the choir and sometimes my mum used to go to church and if she did, we had to go to church with her, and that was it. Sometimes I resented it. We used to go up onto Bredon hill and play, used to love it, used to be an orchard on the left hand side before we started to climb up the hill, we'd climb over the gate and nick the apples and take them with our meal. We never got caught. We used to go scrumping. There was an orchard used to have Worcester Permains, they were beautiful apples, we used to go in and nick them, we used to go over the fence. Kids don't do it today do they? Today they've got everything put in front of them. Years ago we had no toys to play with because our folks couldn't afford to buy them, we had to make do, play hide and seek, fox and hounds

Bengeworth Guides.

and all sorts of games we used to play. One used to be the fox and we all used to hide our faces and he used to go away and hide and we used to have to find him.

Isabelle Beckley, born 1915

They had Their Own Playroom

Friends of mine had their own room, you see, their own playroom and we used to play up there more than play outside. There was a piano and records. We played Ludo as well. We played quite a lot of tennis. At the back of where I lived we had a huge paddock. It was enclosed, very private and we used to stay there. We occasionally played hopscotch – but if you put that on a pavement you used to have to rub it off!

Betty Jones, born 1910

Tree Houses

We had a big conker tree outside our house. We had to have it cut down. They'd come in our garden. I played conkers. My brother used to bake them in the oven to get them hard. We had a medlar tree in our garden. It's a fruit. They were round with a stalk on the top – like an apple but very small. We had a tree house in it. Our mother used to say 'Come on in – where are you? Up in that tree house again?' You could see all over Evesham. It was made of coats and bags. We didn't have a rope or a ladder, we climbed up into the tree. We used to make houses with dirt. Scatter dirt round the garden, make a house – a flat one – like a plan. Me and my sisters used to play in it. We played all sorts of games. Hide and seek, we used to hide in

the coal house. Some in the coal house, some in the shed, some in with the hens. They'd often get out and I'd have to catch them.

Doris Hartland, born 1918

Rat-Tatting

We used to have a game of hide and seek and of course at the bottom of Church Street we had what they called Jubilee Seat, square like with a horse chestnut tree in the middle and we all used to congregate there and then we used to play games. We all used to run in different directions. Some of us went we so far, then as soon as this person went to find us, we ran back and laid under the seats, on the slab floor the seat was on, to stop there till they come back. We used to do the same, rat-tatting the doors or tying one knocker because the doors were so close together. You tie both the knockers and let the one knocker go and if they opens their door then the other knocker goes and that's how it was.

Florence Edna Elizabeth Hunt, born 1927

Playing Tricks

We used to go out at nights and put a button on a piece of cotton and hang it over somebody's door and stand behind the hedge and pull the cotton and it'd go 'clink, clink'. They'd open the door and look round, nobody there – such things as that. We used to put a parcel on the edge of the road, all tied up nice and tidy with a label on it. Somebody'd come riding along, because it was mostly bikes then. We'd be behind the hedge with a long piece of string tied to this parcel and they'd go to pick it up and it jumped out of the road. We used to get some curses. We had the best days really, a lot of things those days we don't do today, they were mischievous, but not trouble making or anything like that.

Bernard Hunt, born 1922

China Doll

My sister had a lovely china doll and it had a christening gown on it – and I swapped it for something else and I had to go back and get it. It wasn't my doll to do it with. She hasn't forgotten it to this very day! We thought it was really daring to jump in someone's hedge or knock on their window.

Sandra Grady, born 1943

Melting Doll

My sister had a doll – and I always remember my brother laying her in front of the coal fire and he melted. It was wax. My mother wasn't pleased because it made a damn fine mess on the coconut matting.

Doris Greenhalf, born 1913

Mr Ward's Blue Bag

Mr Ward used to come round with his van once a week with everything on it and we'd have a packet of crisps and while he was in somebody's house we'd go and help ourselves to the vinegar on the back of his van. He sold everything – pots, pans, paraffin, brasso – the pots were hanging down – it was more like an ironmongers on wheels. If you wanted something he'd get it for you next week. You could get brooms and blue bag, that was for whitening the whites. You'd put it in the last rinse. One day we went down the Silk Mills and there were bees down there and we upset one of the hives. The bees went in my hair, my cousins got them off me and then they tied this blue apron round my head and took me off home. Mother put this blue bag all over my head where I'd been stung. I had a blue head for a bit.

Sandra Grady, born 1943

Swimming to the Orchard

We used to go scrumping – the ambition of every kid, it was to get to learn to swim, quick, so we could swim across the river. There was a wonderful orchard there. Apples, plums, pears, the lot you know. And we always, when we could swim, we used to get across there and stuff them all round here, down the front of our bathing costumes and swim back. Those all over suits, I think they were great. We never got caught, it was every kid's ambition to learn to swim, so we could get over there and get a bellyful of fruit. But of course, we used to lose quite a few of them swimming back, you know, but there was always enough to enjoy them.

Nick Capaldi, born 1913

I was a Tomboy

I'd help dad in the garden at this time of year. He'd be planting his new potatoes. I'd

Ethel Marion Heritage aged eight, with her brother, Frank.

put them in the holes, making sure the eyes were sticking up. He'd make the holes and I'd follow behind. In the summer months we'd play in the coppice down Badsey Brook. We'd take some bread and some water and we'd scrump the rest – tomatoes, fruit, apples. If we got caught, they'd just tell us to clear off. They'd tell your dad. We only used to take one or two, not a lot. They'd tell dad and he'd say, 'You were on someone else's ground' and we'd say 'Yes' 'Don't do it again' And we'd go back. I was a proper tomboy. I wasn't a lady at all. Dad said he always had to get me ready last. If he got Marina ready she'd just sit there, but I'd get dirty before everyone else was ready. They used to dare me to do things. Once they dared me to do a somersault of the back of a lorry. I did and I broke my arm! I got a good hiding for doing it.

Sandra Grady, born 1943

A Sip of Mild and Bitter

Every night when I lived with my Gran I used to have to go and fetch her a jug of mild and bitter. When I used to come back with this jug, there were some sheds where they used to keep the traps for the horses and I used to stop and have a quick sip out of this jug – I reckon I was only about eleven when I had my first sip out of the jug – and I never told her, but, well it was only a sip.

Dorothy May Sollis, born 1921

Fry the Bed

My granny was only a little tiny lady but she was a force to be reckoned with. My God, she'd have the pants off you!

In the winter my grandfather used to have a warming pan – or he'd put a brick in the oven. And she'd say, 'Fry the bed granddad!' It was a big copper warming pan. It was my job Saturday morning to clean the brass, after I'd done the shopping. Then I had 6d a week doing the shopping and I used to be allowed to spend 3d. Mother used to put 3d to it and buy a Saving Stamp. I had that money for years and years. I used to spend 3d: penny for the pictures, pennyworth of monkey nuts and a penny pomegranate – people don't know what they are. There used to be stalls in the market all on a Saturday night. My father used to bring us a threepenny Easter Egg – Cadburys. It was a big one for 3d.

Doris Greenhalf, born 1913

Helping with the Chores

My dad always kept a leather strap about 2 to 3 inches wide, he used to have it up by his chair and if we was naughty we was gone upstairs like lightning. We knew what that meant. He never hit us, but it learned us to do as we were told. As soon as it got dark at night we used to have our tea and that. We didn't have homework in them days from school, we used to go to bed and that. Up in the morning, got ready for school. As we got older, mother went to work on the ground, she used to give us so much jobs to do before we went to school. One would wash up, one would wipe up, we used to have to wash the floor over, there were no carpets in them days, all peg rugs and flagstones. It was hard work in them days. The washing was done in an old fashioned fire, get the water up first and light a fire. There used to be a sort of flat roofed place put on the back of the house and we used to have the furnace in the corner.

Florence Edna Elizabeth Hunt, born 1927

Scrubbing the Saucepans

I used to have to clean the saucepans once a week. We didn't have stainless steel and stuff like that. They all used to have to be scrubbed. The lids used to have to be cleaned with brick dust – they were tin lids. They got discoloured from being on the range. And I used to have to help in the garden, fairly big garden we had. My dad kept ducks and a few hens and I used to have to collect the eggs. But we had a cockerel

who was very spiteful, he used to run at you, I didn't like that!

Phyllis Reay, born 1914

Eggs in Isinglass

My aunt had a bed and breakfast and she used to not pickle eggs, but keep them fresh. She used to get these big buckets and put something in – Isinglass I think it is, and they put this in the bucket, drop the eggs in gently and they float. You can fill the bucket as long as there's a bit around each egg. I used to hate it. She used to say: 'Go down the cellar Honor and get me four eggs'. You had that when eggs were short and I used to have to put my hand in this bucket and it's all gooey, like – ever put your hand in wallpaper paste? It's like that exactly, the

Vine Street, 1930.

Vicarage Court.

hand and carry it and walk round the village like that. I read in the paper one day where a milk boy had been struck by lightning. It hit the milk can and hit him and that was it. So when it thundered and I went out milking, I used to get my hankie and wrap it round the milk handles. Don't know if it'd've done any good though. I was about eight or nine I suppose. I did it right up till I was eleven years old and I had to leave the school at Wick and go to Pershore High School and I couldn't do it because I wouldn't be back in time for school. I used to deliver the milk, come back, go into the barn and chop logs for the furnace, where they used to scald all the milk churns and cans and everything. I used to have to put enough logs and sticks there so they could start in the morning. At night I used to come back and go deliver milk again and then come back and get any more logs they might want and I think I used to get 1s 6d a week for that. I never had much illness at all.

Bernard Hunt, born 1922

same – I used to hate it. You take them out and you fry them, boil them, poach them, do what you like, they kept. Of course there were no fridges then.

Honor Clements, born 1915

Delivering Milk

We lived at Wick most of my life, because my father was head gardener at the estate and I used to have to get up at six o'clock in the morning and take the milk round the villages and the big houses, before breakfast, so they could have fresh milk for breakfast. I used to have six cans in my

Adolescence

Out with the Boys

We went out with the boys, used to go dancing, we used to ask permission to go and they used to say no, so we used to sneak out. Parents aren't so strict these days are they, to what they used to be years ago? My parents were very strict. My mother was lovely. She used to take our part of course. My father was very strict – if he said we had to be in by nine o'clock it was nine – not quarter past, or we were in trouble. He was very strict but he was good. I had two sisters. Many times I came in late and he used to lock the door and go to bed. He always went to bed early as he was a groom and had to be up early in the morning. His motto was early to bed early to rise, so he used to lock the door and he used to go to bed. Outside our front door was like a porch and I used to climb up this porch and in through the bedroom window. My sisters did the same. I was the eldest. I had a sister, Phyllis, and a younger sister, Audrey, I was eleven years older than her. Father knew we used to climb up the porch, we had to go through their bedroom to get to ours as we only had a two bedroom house. The girls had one room and they had the other and we had to go through his bedroom to get to our bedroom. He used to get up in the morning and we used to be in our beds and he'd say, 'If I'd've had my gun and I'd've seen you coming through that window last night, I'd've shot you.' I don't think he would have, but he used to say it.

Isabelle Beckley, born 1915

Biking it to the Dance

Evesham's all right, but I came here early part of the war and been here ever since. I wouldn't like to live in the country now, although they've got better things in the country than they had years ago, because when I was a young girl there was no lights or anything. If you went out it was pitch black dark and if you hadn't got a torch it was tough luck. We hadn't got torches in those days. We walked to dances, or you went on your bike. If you went on your bike you had to scoop your dress up and put a great big safety pin in it. We used to have

fun. We never used to drink. They were very strict years ago. I've been threatened with his [my father's] belt many a time.

Isabelle Beckley, born 1915

No Sex Education

I always remember when I had my first period, I was frightened to death – I didn't know what had happened to me. And my mother saw the stains on my clothes and she said 'You keep away from the boys now!' and I thought what have the boys got to do with this lot? She never told me nothing. I had to learn all about life from older girls at school. We didn't have classes about it like they do now. You had to find out for yourself, didn't you? I don't know whether it's a good thing or not, I suppose it is in some ways. I don't know. Girls used to have illegitimate babies all the time, they used to say 'she ain't the first and she won't be the last', that's what they used to say. I don't think it matters, it's their life – let them get on with it. It's better for the girls these days, when I was a young girl there was nothing. If there was any protection at all, I didn't know about it – I don't know whether the boys did, no-one used to talk about it. We never used to have sex lessons at school or anything like that. We had to learn the hard way.

Isabelle Beckley, born 1915

When the Time Came

I was the eldest of four: two boys and two girls. Well, I went to service. My sister went to service. In them days you wasn't asked, you went to service. Your box was packed, in fact I'd never seen my periods and I always remember it, in them days you had a little terry towelling with the corners turned down and a tape and my mother had to tell me about it, because I didn't know. She had to put in the box you see, for when the time came. You see we were so innocent in them days.

Doris Saunders, born 1913

Helping the Liberals

There were some funny things we used to do as well. It used to be quite exciting when people went to vote. They used to come round trying to get people to vote, I don't know how old I was fifteen, sixteen? And there was a man put up for the Liberal, Senec Davis. The girl I was apprenticed with said they had this group for the younger people to join. So my friend said I think we ought to join that, it might be good. So we went and they wanted us to help, to address envelopes, to send out to people to try and get them to vote. We sat there for hours doing these envelopes and then my father found out what I was doing and he went mad, because he was very Conservative! I was doing quite the wrong thing working with the Liberals. I got into trouble for that! But the Conservatives, they had the same thing for young people – they were called the Imps, so I did join that for a

Waterside.

Polling Day, 1910.

while and that was alright. But politics I never understood and I don't now. I know what I think and what I feel ought to be done, but I don't understand politics.

Phyllis Reay, born 1914

CHAPTER 2

Love and Marriage

Ethel Marion Heritage walking out with a young man in Birmingham, 1934.

Courtship

Lights out at the Regal

We used to tell the time by the Regal Cinema, Jim and I when we were courting. Where we used to say goodnight, we used to be able to see the lights on the Regal go out. And when they went out you knew it was time to go in, which was about ten o'clock, and that was late, very late.

Olive Thould, born 1918

Dark Haired Boy

I was apprenticed to the milliner people at Bengeworth, where the Regal cinema is now, and it was a biggish shop and he [my first husband] was their nephew, he came from Newcastle upon Tyne and these Stubbs, the people I worked for, didn't have any family, but the girls at work, older than me, used to talk about this Eric. My name was Smith before I was married and they used to say, 'Just right for you!' I always said I would only go out with a dark haired boy you see.

Phyllis Reay, born 1914

Hobnail and Clinker

We met at Broadway at a dance. It was love at first sight. It was two or three times I'd been to the dance and watched her and all the rest of it. I wasn't much of a dancer and I didn't get up much so I thought, I'll try it and that's how we started. What we used to call 'hobnail and clinker'. In the old days the boys they used to have nothing but these boots, steel tipped and toed, and they used to go everywhere – they called them hobnailed boots and all that. Because when you went to dances they used to say you're going to the 'hobnail and clinker' because your boots made a bang on the floor. I lived in Bengeworth then and the first time I took her home to Willesley, because I didn't know it was blackout then, they still hadn't got street lights, and I went up to this road and the pool's down here opposite. I came flying down this road and my lights picked up this row of stones and I thought this was the curb of the road, but it wasn't, it was the side of the duck pond and I went in, bike and all. It was the first time I had worn my demob suit. It was said that if you fell in the duck pond, you were made mayor of Willesley for twelve months!

I made that trip to Willesley three times a week and weekends and I used to try and race the storms back home, but we had good times. It was not until the latter days of our courtship that I bought a car – a little Morris Minor thing. I bought it out of Evesham market when they had a car sale – £850 quid or something. It was a lovely little car, we used to go everywhere in it.

Bernard Hunt, born 1922

Watching a Football Match

Well, I was working at the hospital with my sister and we were very friendly with a young girl that worked along the common and she was an upholsterer at Fowlers in the High Street. And her brother used to be a carpet layer for Fowlers and we used to go with Winnie down to her home and my dad used to send her parents rabbits you know, because we spent our spare time down there. This one night Perce had got a colleague, Harold Street, that worked with him, and Fred Turner from the town hall, they were in the boys brigade together. They were in the boys brigade you know, all these boys and Fred said we had a dance last night at the public hall and so I shall be having an early night, 'May I walk you back up to the hospital?' So that's how we started.

Fred brought me up from the common that night and he was outside the hospital when I was off duty in the nurses home the next day, I didn't have much time out really, Sunday afternoons I think it was and I always had to be in before dark. Always, my word yes! And I came out thinking Winnie was out there, instead it was Fred Turner and he said, 'I should change your shoes if I were you, we're going down the meadows and

Evesham Floods.

we're going to a football match and the grass is very long and it's very wet.' So I had to go and put my boots on. And so he always expected me to go to a blessed football match with him.

Any road, before we were married, it was 1923 when the Robins went to Crystal Palace, I was in service at Mr Beales, Mrs Beales and I said, 'Could I have the day off?' They said, 'What do you want it for?' and I said, 'I got the chance to go to Crystal Palace with the Robins football match.' 'Oh!', Mr Beale said, 'you go!' So we had the day off that day. We had a lovely time out.

Catherine Maude Turner, born 1902

That's the One I Want

She turned round and said 'Oh, here's a couple of chaps I know, coming'. They came up and started talking. The river was in flood and they said 'Shall we go down and see the floods?' So I said, 'Alright'. I didn't know much about this, I was totally innocent, so off we went. We had to go through the park, round the park. It was dark. So then we went and paired up. I had this great big tall bloke. I could have married him and ended up with a house and God knows what … look what I missed. Poor George! We were friends right up to the end. So I said to Doris – I don't want this George, I don't like him! That's the one I want – the one you've got and I'm going to marry him! And I did! About four or five years after, but I still married him when the war broke out.

Olive Thould, born 1918

Marriage

Our Own Act

I met my wife; she was a member of the band. She could play, but better than that, she could sing – had a wonderful voice. In my opinion she was the star of the band. We did this British tour, after we'd finished the continental tour, we came back to England. I went down to Southend on Sea, because I'd got very friendly with her during the tour, I went down to Southend to see her father. In those days, they don't do it now, but in those days you had to see the young lady's father if you wanted to go any further, you know, which I did. They said, 'Don't be in such a hurry to go, its nice here in Southend on Sea,' and her father said to me 'What do you want to go back and join the band for? You admit she's the star of the show and you're the best player of the show. You're better than the man that runs the thing. Why don't you do your own act?' And anything we wanted, he paid for it. At the same time I'd got friendly with the manager at the Rivoli Cinema, he was a concertina player, but he wanted to play the accordion and he'd got a small accordion. So I gave him some lessons on the accordion and he was getting on very well and after I'd been rehearsing our act in the ballroom for a couple of weeks, her mum made the costume for her, she made a frilly skirt, with all coloured ribbons on, a satin blouse with

The Capaldis in their first costumes as a duo.

Mr and Mrs Grove, Crest Hall, Harrington.

puffed sleeves with a bolero, a little waistcoat. Her mum made the lot and her costume was beautiful. She made a bolero for me, in velvet trimmed with gold, and a blouse but the trousers were just normal black evening dress trousers with a sash. It looked very good, quite honestly.

Nick Capaldi, born 1913

A Banner in Byker

We were playing at a place called Byker. We decided to get married so I went to see the priest in Newcastle and it was all arranged. The day we got married we were of course playing, did a performance that night and towards the end of the performance, a big notice came down, about that width and almost across the stage 'Just Married'. Of course, the audience went absolutely bonkers.

Nick Capaldi, born 1913

Watching the Cricket

I was married at Fladbury and my husband was a churchgoer and I remember the parson saying to us, we shall miss you at church. We had a little do in the parish room at Moore, then rang the bells at Fladbury because Den was a bell ringer, and I tell you what, oh Den was a gardener and he worked in the Manor at Cropthorne, as a private gardener and she was mean, and all he got was one day when we was married and do you know how we spent it? We went to Worcester to the cricket, because we was cricket fans. That was our honeymoon, it was Easter Monday. I love the cricket. I like all sport, tennis and all that. Poor people didn't play tennis.

Doris Saunders, born 1913

Lace or Turn-ups

When we were married, it was 1943 and oh, didn't Gladys have to do some queueing and scampering about to try and get something to wear! It was all on tokens and I had to have a lace dress because my husband wanted a suit and he couldn't have no turn-ups on his trousers, so he went to Hepworths on the corner and he had his trousers made that much longer so that I could do him a turn-up. But if he did that then he couldn't have a breast pocket. If I'd have had an ordinary dress we would have lost a lot of coupons and he wouldn't have had his suit so I had to have a lace dress because there was no coupons on lace.

Gladys Davis, born 1911

Coupons for the Dress

I had two husbands. One died, then I married again five or six years after. I worked with the first one during the war. The war had just broken out, I was twenty-six, and I worked with him, that's how I met him. My wedding day – it was coupons, wasn't it? You had to find eighteen coupons for the dress alone, then you wanted shoes and all manner, the veil – eighteen coupons and it was twenty a month. It wasn't much because you'd got underclothes and stockings and all, and shoes, all came out of the coupons.

Ethel Marion Heritage, born 1913

Married in May

I met my wife, Miss Higley, before the war. We got married in May and we'd been married twelve months when war broke out in September. I was working in a shop in Cheltenham at the time and I came into Evesham, naturally, to get married. We got

Ruben Clark and Clara Bishop, 1923.

married in the registry office. You didn't have what you call best clothes.

Wilfred John Ayres, born 1916

Fifty Shilling Tailor

I didn't have an elaborate wedding, I didn't want one. I had a blue suit with a gold lining and I had it from the fifty shilling tailors. I had a pair of navy blue shoes and a little blue hat. I wasn't married in church; I was married at the registry office – much to my mother's disgust!

Mrs Townley, born 1915

Treated like Royalty

I had a dress made for the wedding. Where the Regal Cinema is, now the lady I worked for, Mrs Beale, she said, 'Maude, I shouldn't be dressed in white', she said, 'because it's a waste of money. I should have a dress that you can use for Sundays afterwards'. So I had a grey alpaca dress made, edged with pink, silver lace down the front and round the waist. Then I had a hat made in grey underlined with pink and my sisters, two sisters had navy blue hats with blue underneath and my bridesmaid, she had a blue dress on with silver grey lace on the top of that. And then I had a mauve, deep Parma violet topcoat put on top. When we went to Oxford we went to a tea room and there was still rice on me, I'd still got rice in me hat and that and the folks treated us as if we were royalty at this teahouse we went to.

Catherine Maude Turner, born 1902

Second Hand Furniture

I had a white dress for my wedding, and my husband's sister and my sister was bridesmaids, and we had a little do in the parish room at Lower Moore which my dad paid for. But as I say, we went to the Smithfield at Evesham and bought all our furniture second hand. I had to wait till the kids growed up and I worked to, you know, get the things I wanted, and today they has it all before they start.

Doris Saunders, born 1913

Not Without my Glasses

I wouldn't be married in white because I wore glasses and in those days there weren't many people wearing glasses. In my day, if you wore white with a veil, you took your glasses off. I was practically blind without my glasses. My mother wouldn't speak to me for a week because I wouldn't be married in white. You know Tewkesbury Abbey, it's a heck of a long way from the gates to the alter. I could see myself falling half a dozen times going down there. So my dress was airforce blue and it had a stand up collar and the whole of the bodice was closely smocked, it was very heavy, actually, and a full skirt and the matching frill at the bottom, brown shoes and I had King Alfred daffodils in my bouquet.

Honor Clements, born 1915

A Bowlful of Dahlias

I was married on 22 September 1926 and Mrs Potter next door, she picked all her

Mr and Mrs Taylor, Grandma Panter, Frank Moss.

dahlias and put it in our hedge down the middle of, between our houses and she put a great big bowlful outside our front door under the porch where mother stood. So when I opened the front door with our dad, all these flowers were out there and the village people all gave me simple little presents, like a tray and this, that and the other, a dish or something, different little things. When we came out of our house they throwed rice at us, they hadn't got confetti because it was out in the country and I said next time I shall want something different, I don't want rice, it don't half hurt. But there never was a next time.

Catherine Maude Turner, born 1902

Married in the Snow

It's the first and the last; we shan't never pick up with no one else. We've been married fifty-three years on 15 February. It was 1947, deep snow, we couldn't have a photographer out at the church because of the snow. We had to go to him a week afterwards and I know when we come from church it was on a bit of a slope, and if we hadn't got hold of one another we'd've been down. We managed to save ourselves.

Florence Edna Elizabeth Hunt, born 1927

The Taxi couldn't Get Up There

When we went, the taxi couldn't get up there – it was thick with ice. We had to get out of the taxi and walk up to the church; '47 was one of the bad winters, it lasted come March.

Bernard Hunt, born 1922

Mass in a Tin Hut

Well look, this is the Royal Wedding, now I worked at the hospital when I was sixteen and the Royal Wedding took place in 1907. This is Wood Norton and eight of my folks worked in that building – that's Wood Norton. They had a chapel built in the grounds of Wood Norton for this Royal Wedding for people to come up from all over the world to this wedding. But when it came to the wedding it wasn't consecrated, so they had to move into an old tin hut for the wedding. There was no Roman Catholic church in Evesham until 1913 and my relation used to drive the priest from the monastery in Broadway to bring the priest from the monastery up to give the Duc d'Orleans Holy Mass on a Sunday morning.

They used to have one of those little round tubs with the pony and Lou King sat in the one side and the priest sat in the other to bring this little pony up from Wood Norton to Broadway, the six miles.

Catherine Maude Turner, born 1902

Childbirth

Fetch Evelyn

The district nurse used to live in the village. Mother used to help her. She bought a lot of babies into the world. They used to say, 'Go and fetch Evelyn' and many the time the baby was born before the nurse had time to

THE ROYAL WEDDING. WAITING TO SEE ROYALTY ARRIVE AT EVESHAM

The Royal Wedding, 1908.

Nailers Row, Bengeworth, c. 1930.

get there. She said it was surprising the people you thought would be prepared for a baby weren't and she'd have to dash off and get sheets and things.

Sandra Grady, born 1943

Gas and Air

The first two children I went into hospital with, the others I had at home. The last one, when I had it at home, the gas and air ran out and he [my husband] had to bike from Hampton to the nurse's place in town to pick up some gas and air and come back and I didn't need it when he got back, because the baby was nearly born.

Florence Edna Elizabeth Hunt, born 1927

Barrel of Cider

We had a little house at Great Cumberton: 3s 6d a week it was, and I always remember when I was carrying my first, David, my baby. You know you gets cravings, well the farmer gives Den this little barrel of cider and it was down the garden in the shed and do you know, I used to go down, the neighbour used to laugh. I had a craving for this cider and I was going down there with a cup to fetch this cider out. And I remember when David was born, I was in labour all night and I'd done a line of washing and my husband kept saying, 'You shouldn't have done that washing, that's what it was'. Anyhow I said, 'Go and fetch Bet', because he went to school with Bet, the girl next door. And he fetches her and she says, 'Oh Den,' she says 'Doris has been in labour all

Four Corners, c. 1900.

night, fetch that nurse quick'. And she was only just in time. I always laugh because she said to me, 'Well, good job you didn't send for me before, because I've been along Hopney Cottage and in the end I had to give her a slap'. Been screaming all night. I mean I had my three kids, no doctor, just the nurse, at home and I remember the little nurse said to me 'I should go to Hodges and get your pram and your cot, but don't pay for it and if anything happens you can not pay for it.' So I did. I never had no trouble at all.

Doris Saunders, born 1913

Tips From Two Kings

My wife's first marriage broke up in London so she came to Evesham to stop with her sister for a week and she thought she'd get a job. So she got a job as a barmaid at the Rose and Crown – of course I used to go in there and that's where I met her. We started going out and it went from there. Then I was doing the Covent Garden trips and she liked London so on her day off she used to come too. [Before she came to Evesham] she was in service with Lord and Lady Allendale in London in Hyde Park Corner. There used to be three big houses there. One was the Rothchilds, one was the Allendales and in the middle was the Duke of York who later became King George VI. The Queen and Princess Margaret used to come in the kitchen when my wife was working there and ask if they could have permission to use the stove to make toffee.

King Edward the VIII, when he abdicated used to go there, as my wife said, she had two 10 bob tips from two kings in one week, from the king of Bulgaria and Edward VIII, the Duke of Windsor.

Joe Sherwood, born 1923

CHAPTER 3

Home Life

Floods at Port Street.

Groceries and Gardening

Violets in the Garden

My father only used to go into Oxford once a month to fetch his pension and buy his grocery. Well, they got a well there and they used to put all the butter and different things they wanted to keep, he only bought the grocery once a month and everything that had got to be kept it was hung in this well.

He always kept a pig to manure his garden ... and he used to grow the most marvellous violets all down the one side of a long garden and potatoes on the other and every March he used to get these violets up and he used to cut it right away; they used to grow just like strawberry roots. And he used to put bits of stuff in the ground like two fingers, two roots and the stalks and the flowers and the scent was just out of this world. But it was the manure and the house refuse that was all buried in that garden and fed the potatoes and he changed it every year. Each year potatoes one side, violets the other and we were all out there, five or six of us, picking these violets and he used to take them into Oxford into Webbs and they used to sell them to the students, the Oxford students at the colleges.

The only enemy of the violet is the red spider and the red spider eats round the edge of the leaf so when they do that he used to have to use an ivy leaf to put behind the violets because he couldn't put a bitten, soiled leaf behind in the bunches, he used to use ivy leaves. Oh, hundreds and hundreds and hundreds of bunches they used to have and oh, the scent was beautiful.

At the bottom of the garden, was a running stream with watercress. We had

Church Yard, Evesham.

lots of watercress and one day Aunt Em had a party and a nurse came to tea and Evelyn was only a little girl and the nurse said, 'Aren't you going to have some of this watercress?' Evelyn said, 'No, that's for you, we can have watercress every day. But that's a treat for you. Mummy said we've got to leave it because we can have it any time'. Aunt Em said, 'Children always tell the truth don't they?'

Catherine Maude Turner, born 1902

Pinching our Plums

I used to go up the garden and pick a few raspberries, a few strawberries, gooseberries and redcurrants. And then we had a whole row of plum trees all up one side, and some apple trees. The kids used to come pinching of course – scrumping. We had a lot of yellow egg plums so they used to pinch them when they were ripe and somebody would have such a bad tummy and wonder why!

Doris Haines, born 1913

Feeding the Pig

Two of us, my husband and someone else had a pig between them during the war. We had to take it turns to feed this wretched thing and cook the food. They weren't handsome things – you had to give proper attention to what you were doing. In the old farm kitchens the sides used to be hung up in the kitchens and then they had the hams, all in muslin bags.

Betty Jones, born 1910

The Pig Club

There were so many in what they call the pig club, and you see, you each draw a number in turn. If you were first you were lucky, you had the seeing to it, the pig, last. It was a fair share and everybody had the same. It was hard work though when you had quite a way to go to see to it, to tend it. But it was worth it though, well worth it.

Doris Hartland, born 1918

The Rats'd Get Them

I used to have one or two hens and when one got broody I was afraid to put the proper eggs under her you see, because the rats'd have them. You used to have these china eggs and I'd put the china eggs under them and when the three weeks were up I'd buy some day old chicks, see them advertised in the paper. But you'd got to be very careful, you get your hand under her and slip out an egg and put a chick under her. When she started clucking you knew that she'd take to them.

Gladys Davis, born 1911

Washing

A Tap in the House

I was born out in the Lenches. My father died at thirty-nine, he was very young and me mother was left with three little kids, see. He was at Elmley, where he was a stockman and lived in a tied cottage, and

Cottages adjoining Northwich Hotel.

we had to get out. That's when we went to Sedgeberrow, we had a little old cottage. That was a place, there was one tap outside for five houses. The toilet was a shed up the garden with a bucket, no electric, nothing like that. It was candles and oil lamps. My mother had no social services, no social security. She got 10s for herself, widow's pension, and 5s for we three kids and 7s 6d a week for the rent of the old house. Then we went into a council house when they built the council houses in 1932, I was nine then, we thought we was in clover. 'Oh, we've got a tap in the house!' No hot water mind, but a tap in the house. We had a bathroom, it was cold water, but we had a furnace, we had to light a fire under the boiler to get hot water. Then bucket it into the bath. The loo was a bucket, not a water toilet. That wasn't fitted in till years after. Course, them days nobody got much.

Joe Sherwood, born 1923

Using the Dolly Tub

My mother didn't work – they didn't in those days, they used to bring up the kids, do the cooking and cleaning and that was it. Washing had to be done by hand; there were no washing machines in those days. My mother used to have a dolly tub, a tub with a stick with like three prongs on the bottom and she used to do this with the sheets in the dolly tub and I've turned the mangle many a time for her when she's been putting the sheets through. It was hard work in those days.

Isabelle Beckley, born 1915

Monday Was Washday

We had a long yard at the back of our houses, because you had to walk over the yard to get to the toilet. So my mother always did the washing on a Monday and she'd put a line across the yard and when she'd got the washing in, she'd take the line down, because they took it in turns to have a line and because the kids liked to go out into the yard and play. So anyway, she'd go and light the copper, outside, there wasn't room in the house, you had to do it outside. So she'd light the copper to get the water hot. And she'd use soda, handfuls of soda she put in the water – we didn't have powder in them days, it's good for washing, soda, anyway. And then she'd take everything. She'd take the sheets off the beds, she'd take the tablecloths, the clothes, she'd have a general wash up, everything had to be washed on a Monday. As fast as she got one lot out, she'd do another lot. She was all day doing it. On Sunday she always cooked enough food to fry up on the Monday, because she was too busy to cook a meal on the Monday, so Sunday she always did extra. Then she had relays with her washing, one lot in, one lot out. Now we always had a tablecloth, but we didn't have a tablecloth Monday because it was in the wash, so she used to put newspaper on the table, our scrubbed table, so it wouldn't show the football pitch! Then after she'd finished washing she used to use the water and she used to scrub the floors – so imagine our kitchen, it was only a little kitchen and it had flagstones, those big flagstones, that's what

was on the floor and maybe a peg rug, because we used to make peg rugs with the old bits of material in the winter. So she used to use the water to scrub all the floors, even outside in the yard got scrubbed – the water with the soda in.

[If it was raining] She'd still peg it out, she pegged the first lot out and if it was still raining she put the second lot in the bath and let it stop there. Then at night when we went to bed, she'd put it round the fire, we had a guard round the fire, she put it on there after we'd gone to bed. A lot of our washing was dried indoors and she was always hand washing, pants and socks, you know. Every day she did a bit of hand washing – I'm talking about the big wash – you know – sheets and pillowcases and such. Little things she'd just rub through and put them round the boiler outside, at night put them on the guard, they'd be dry the next morning.

Dorothy May Sollis, born 1921

Making Starch

We used to make starch in a bowl. You bought the starch, it was in little pieces and then you put the cold water on it until it had all dissolved, then you put the boiling water over it, stirred it and used it. But it was horrible! You put your things in the bowl of starch, squeezed it out and hung it out to dry. You ironed it while it was still damp.

Mrs Townley, born 1915

Snow-White Cloth

My mother used to say – I'm not eating off that cloth! I mean we were married and we'd invited her, but 'I'd rather have bread and cheese off a snow-white cloth than a banquet off a dirty cloth!' And perhaps it was only one little spot. And do you know it used to take hours to do those cloths, because they had to be starched, they were big and you had to pull them into shape. The irons used to have to stand on the hob, you had a holder for them. And my mother always spat on the iron and if it shot off it was hot. But the cloths looked beautiful. They were all patterned, like a watermark. You ironed them and they shone. We'd do the ironing on an ordinary table. You made a pad out of old towels. Mind you if you creased them you had that crease on everything you ironed.

Honor Clements, born 1915

Pumping the Water

We used to have a windmill up there just near the brook, Telford brook, and during the early days of the war, petrol was that tight it was my job to start the engine up and pump. I think that windmill was put up by some men I worked with, just after they finished in the First World War because in those days it belonged to someone called George Littler. When the war was over and they come back they fitted this big windmill up as the first step towards modernization on the farm to fix the water supply up. I used to pump this 1,500 gallons of water with the windmill into the tanks at the farm. I supplied all the livestock and all the farm buildings and the washing and everything and then there was a pipe run from the farm up to the cottage. When the floods were on it was like cocoa coming out of the tap. It was awful, even when you boiled it and

filtered it through mutton cloth, but we survived it.

Before that, the water used to have to come out of a well between a set of four houses and very often in the summer it used to get pretty dry and they used to come round with a big water tanker from Pershore and you used to have to pay a penny a bucket for the water. You used to have to do the washing and the housework and the drinking and everything.

Bill Atkinson, born 1921

Food

Always Rice Pudding

There were no electric cookers; it was all cooked by the fireplace in the little kitchen come dining room that we had, a little range. She (mother) used to make her cakes and everything in the oven there. We used to have a roast of some sorts every Sunday and then Monday it was cold meat and fry up, vegetables left from Sunday and always rice pudding because it was washday Monday and that was the easiest thing to do. I forget what we used to have Tuesday, but we used to have stew once a week, I remember that.

Isabelle Beckley, born 1915

Pig's Trotters

We used to have tripe and onions and pigs trotters. It's still known that if you make a good stew, it's no good unless you put a pig's trotter in. Because you've got all that solid jelly and the flavour is beautiful. When I lived at Bishampton I got friendly with this farmer and his wife and he used to say to me, 'Kate, if I get some trotters, will you cook them for me' – his wife wouldn't do it for him. He said, 'I'd rather have that than the best cut of the pig'. It's all gluey stuff inside, you get sticky fingers, but you can always lick them. You eat them with your fingers and all the bones come apart – there's no elegance in it! But it was really satisfying.

Sylvia Hickenbothan, born 1913 in conversation with Kate Spilsbury, born 1911

Fish and Chips

If we had fish and chips, my golly that was a treat I'll tell you, because somebody had to go down to Tewkesbury to get that and that was five miles away. If anyone was going to Tewkesbury, they always used to come and say, 'We're going to Tewkesbury, do you want any chips?' and they used to bring loads back for people, fish and chips from the fish and chip shop. They were ever so good. They all did it in their turn. There used to be a bus that went down twice a week, I think, three times – mornings, afternoons and evenings. It used to come back at nine o'clock and that was just right for supper for fish and chips. It was a great treat. If there was any left, it was never thrown away, but was eaten cold the next day. We never wasted food.

Isabelle Beckley, 1915

Supper at Nine O'clock

There was always a meal on the table by about five o'clock, but in the summer we didn't eat till about nine o'clock because dad would come home and bring something, new peas or something from work, or it would be off the garden. He'd work until about six or seven and by the time he'd biked from Bower Hill to Badsey, which was about three miles, he was ready for his supper. When mother worked at the hospital the first one in would start supper. It was always nice to go home. There was a fire in the grate, it was like a range we had, and it always smelt nice. She'd do all the cooking and the baking. Sunday she used to bake cakes and scones, and make trifles. And on her day off she'd do that as well. The cooker was grey, there was a chimney going up, and there was an oven one side and a grate the other side and you pulled the flap down and there was the grate, then you lifted that off. They were built into the council houses in the '50s. We had ours taken out and we had a proper fireplace there when we had the cooker in the kitchen. This was in the living room you see. It was a bit like an Aga. It was nice to sit on in the winter! And mother could air her washing over the top.

Sandra Grady, born 1943

Stone Larder

Most houses had a walk-in larder and the width of it was taken up with stone, thick with stone. It was always cold in there; you could keep butter there in the height of summer. Then you had a window, no glass, just thin, didn't allow anything through. At first they had just ordinary stone, then later they brought in marble, it wasn't that expensive then.

Honor Clements, born 1915

Cake on Fridays

We never used to sit at the table or eat, before both my parents were seated. My boys never sat down till I was seated. And on Fridays, I made cakes all week, but on Fridays I used to treat everyone. My father and my husband and my two sons used to love doughnuts, so I used to buy them on a Friday, for teatime, but they would never touch anything until I'd had mine.

Honor Clements, born 1915

Rhubarb and Sugar

My treats were a saucer with a bit of sugar in and the end of a rhubarb stick and you'd dip the rhubarb in the sugar.

Sylvia Hickenbothan, born 1913

Making Toffee

One of the things we used to do, we had a long spoon and we'd get some butter and some sugar and put it in the fire and it'd bubble up and make toffee. We could only do it sometimes when mother was out and she'd come in and sniff: 'Now what have you been up to?' We used to have to hide the spoon and everything else!

Kate Spilsbury, born 1911

Orange Boxes

Apples weren't sorted the way they are now – you just said you got a good apple or a good orange. You'd pay a ha'penny for an orange that was going rotten and you'd peel it on the way to school to get the best bits. An orange was a real treat. And we used to have the skipping ropes off the orange crates; they were a special yellow. And the crates they came in, we'd use them, we'd paper them and use them for seats in the house or for beside your bed, you'd put a shelf in and a little table cover over and they'd look real nice, real smart! Everyone was always after an orange box.

Kate Spilsbury, born 1911

Evesham Plums

They used to pick the Evesham plums when they were still a bit green, before they get yellow. The Pershore eggplum, is similar to the Evesham, but they have a bluey colour. They crossed it with another one and developed the Evesham one.

We used to bottle them in Kilner jars and store them for the winter. You put them in clear water, or you can make a syrup and pour that in the jar – I used to because I had two sons and they liked everything sweet! And do you know what we used to use to seal the plums? Fat. You melt pure fat, like lard, it's got to be pure, and you pour it over the top and it stays on the top because the plums are cold and it solidifies and as it expands it pushes all the air out and it seals. They used that before the kilner jars. It doesn't change the taste of the plums at all. And when you want to open it, you run a knife around the fat and it comes out solid. The Kilner jars came out in the beginning of

The Charabanc, c. 1900.

the 1930s. We used to get them that airtight you had to put them in hot water to open them. When they first came out you could only get the great big ones. They haven't changed much, glass with rubber seals.

We had an electrical scalder to get the lids off. Yes, but you'd have to careful with that not to lose all your plums!

Honor Clements, born 1915
in converation with Bill Atkinson, born 1921

Lettuce Wine

When the parsnips and stuff like that were ready for digging, my dad used to get a scrubber and steel wool and clean the boiler out and shine it up and make parsnip wine. He used to make 10 gallon of parsnip wine.

I used to make a lot of it one time ... used to be in barrels in the pantry, sometimes the sediment in the bottom of the barrel used to get in the tap, you know, and it would run very slow and my dad used to say, 'Come and blow up that pipe, clear that sediment' and I used to get underneath and blow until I felt it coming, then I used to have a real drink. We made beetroot wine, elderberry wine, elderflower wine; dandelion was another one. That was one of my favourites, used to spend hours and hours picking dandelions, it didn't half take some dandelions to make wine. It was good stuff. The strongest wine I've ever drunk, I didn't make it myself, that was lettuce. I'd already had a drink of beer, it was on the Saturday, had my dinner and all that and went out the back, I thought what am I going to do this afternoon, and my neighbour he says, 'Hey, I've made some wine, do you want to taste it?' 'Ah, yes' – it tasted just like water. I tasted it and I thought that's strong and he says, 'What is it?' and I says 'I have no idea, because there's not much flavour to it.' He said, 'It's lettuce' and I says, 'never heard of it before, not lettuce wine', but it was strong, I can tell you. I didn't do much work that afternoon. We used to go out getting blossom, May flower blossom. You could smell the May flowers when you drank it. Like sweet – you know what may flowers smell like, it was like gin nearly. Beautiful wine, but the trouble was picking the flowers. You only wanted the little petals out of the flower. I tried a lot of it, carrot wine I made a lot of that, carrot whisky, stuff like that. Trouble is you want plenty of room to keep it and it wants to be kept at the right temperature. It

used to be all part of village life, wine making. If you'd got a good barrel of wine on the go, you'd get some chap would come round, 'how are you? I was just passing by and I thought I'd ask how you are. By the way, how's that barrel of wine, is it alright?' Course that was it, he had to taste it.

Bernard Hunt, born 1922

Getting By

Draw and Thread Work

I used to do draw and thread work. You get a piece of linen and draw the threads, you pull them together. You can make patterns

High Street, Evesham.

46

with it. It was done round pillowslips, the open edge of a pillowslip. You pull threads from the linen. You have to have proper material. You use ordinary course linen, not cotton because you can't draw the threads out of cotton. You pull the threads, not right out, but together and you can make patterns, you go round twice, gathering. If you don't want to do too much work you pull more threads It's a bit like smocking, but smocking is closer, and you overstitch the gathering. My mother used to do all the dresses with it. Children's clothes were really popular.

*Honor Clements, born 1915
in conversation with Betty Jones, born 1910*

Mother was a Tailoress

We did rag rugs and wool rugs. Rag rugs used to be great fun. You have sacking, a hessian sack. My mother was a tailoress, so she had loads of scraps of material. We used to draw out a pattern and work the pattern. It was my job to cut the pieces out, mostly the same size. They used to be ever so heavy – dust collectors too!

*Honor Clements, born 1915
in converation with Betty Jones, born 1910*

Clothes to the Pawnshop

Mom had never got nothing really. She bought me clothes till I was a good age really and then I started buying my own. I'd come home from work on a Friday and think, 'Oh, I'll go to the pictures'. Or I may have been courting. I'd go upstairs for my clothes and they'd gone. I'd run downstairs and Mom would say I had to take them to the pawnshop because I hadn't enough money for the rent or the insurance man or something. I'd say, 'Well how much are they in for?' 'Oh – 4d 6s,', something like that, 5 shilling. 'Look here, before the shops shut, run over and get them'. She'd run over and get them and I'd put my suit on. Then on Monday night it'd happen again. I'd have them for the weekend, but then on Monday they're gone. My girl used to come round, to see if we'd go out and I'd say I can't go out, she'd say, 'Why?' 'Look – I'm still in my overalls, my working overalls, my clothes are over the road, at Uncles'. 'Oh, OK, lets go a walk', and we'd go for a walk. You could only get them back on Friday – payday. I gave me mom the wages and she'd get them out, but they were gone on Monday. That's how people lived – well that's how we lived anyway!

Harold Robinson, born 1908

No Women at Funerals

When you had a funeral in those days – women didn't go to funerals – only men. I don't know why. My mother'd always keep mourning stuff and everybody used to come to borrow black for the funeral. The day after she used to send me to fetch it back, in case they flogged it!

Doris Greenhalf, born 1913

My First Bath

I always remember, as a child, the first bath that I ever had. When we lived up the old Rheidol Street, when we were children,

WR Coulters, c. 1900.

The bridge and River Avon at Evesham.

Friday night was bath night. Mother had the tin bath in front of the fire, you know she'd fill it with hot water and then we had to take it in turns and get in each other's water. She'd keep adding a kettle full of water, then the next one had to go, then the next one had to go, right? But it was the same water being hotted up as each one got in it was hotted up with water. The eldest went first, the four boys went first and then it was me, then my sister was last when she was old enough. Of course, by the time I got in there it was three quarters full. My mother didn't start with a lot of water, because she knew she'd got to get us all bathed and then it was what was called medicine night. We had Beecham's pills we had to take because that was for our bowels, to keep our bowels open, they were alright and we always had to have two spoonfuls of cod-liver oil in malt, that was beautiful, I used to love that. Cod-liver oil is horrible, but the malt made it beautiful. We always used to want more, but mother couldn't afford any more. My sister couldn't swallow the Beecham's pills, she could only take what she called slidey pills so she had what they call Carters Little liver pills, she had one of those. We weren't allowed out – Friday night was always bath night and medicine night.

Dorothy May Sollis, born 1921

Gypsy Cures

If you wanted the doctor you had to pay for it. The kids was probably always getting something or another – the normal things that kids get at school, measles, chicken pox and that and you had to report it to the doctor because he had to come out and course your dad had to pay. That was it – full stop!

In the springtime when we got these spots and rashes, mother used to go and get some young stinging nettles and cook them up, and you had them like spinach. That's supposed to clear all your blood out. Used to be a proper Romany gypsy lived by us, down the lane and she used to call in for some water or som'at like that and if anyone of us was under the weather, say 'you give him this' or 'you give him that' and she was right – it used to cure you.

Bernard Hunt, born 1922

Goose Grease

They had a shop down Bridge Street, a chemists? They make all the their own stuff, mix their own stuff. Mother always kept plenty of medicines in anyway. But something for every ailment you had, you could go to this shop and buy something for a few pence. If we had a cold, a chesty cold, Mother had only got to hear us cough or sneeze for a day and at night, out would come the goose-grease. The grease out of a goose, she always saved it, bottled it for a bad chest. Out it would come and a piece of flannel, it had to be flannel on top and you had to keep that on for a day, goose grease and flannel for a chesty cough or cold.

It smelt HORRIBLE! This is where Granny's goose used to come in useful, because she always had a goose at Christmas. They seemed to have everything and to know what to do, if there was anything wrong.

Dorothy May Sollis, born 1921

Brickkiln Street.

The Trumpet Inn, Merstow Green.

Setting Fire to the Chimney

And I used to have to fetch coke. My mum couldn't afford coal, we used to have coke. We had to go up Swan lane, then down quite a big bank to the gas works, that was on the common and we had to go to the gasworks to fetch this coke. We used to take an old pram and it was a shilling for a bag of coke. So we used to ask for a bag of coke and they'd go and shovel it up and it'd still be steaming. They'd put it in a bag and put it on the pram and then when we went back we used to have to pull this pram back up this bank, up the common bank and it was quite a haul because it was quite steep and every day we used to have to fetch some coke for the fire – we had to have it. But we never had a sweep. Our dad used to deliberately set fire to the chimney! Do it on purpose to get rid of the soot. It used to frighten me to death. It used to all come down. He used to bank the fire right up, you couldn't see the top of it and he'd just let it go. And all the sparks and all the soot used to come down. He used to damp sack bags, wet 'em and put 'em down in front of the fireplace. The soot on fire used to land on these sacks. When I grew up I used to be frightened to death my chimney would catch fire. He just let the fire keep going until it burnt itself out. The wall of the chimney, the chimney breast used to get red-hot – he always did it more in the winter than summer!

Dorothy May Sollis, born 1921

CHAPTER 4

Entertainment

The Robins,
1923.

Sport

Evesham United

I never had a Saturday off and I've never been to a football match on a Saturday afternoon but I did eventually get to be on Evesham United's committee and we used to pick the team at the beginning of the week and nobody was paid in those days. Amateurs weren't allowed to receive any money whatever. Today of course it's all money isn't it? I didn't play football, but the team mostly comprised of local fellows. Today they buy players from abroad and all that. We had a certain amount to choose from and they were pretty well all the same every week. They were a good team at the time; they used to play on what they call the Crown Meadow … course it's two meadows now, you know the park – Abbey Park, well the next field to that used to be one large field and when the football team took over they put a fence across the middle to separate, make it into town pitches so you'd be playing on one pitch and somebody else would probably be playing on the other. It was more or less the same team each week. I was on the committee later on and I used to go and be on the gate and take the entrance money. I could see a little of what was going on and I thought, 'Well, he wouldn't be much good next week and we'd try someone else' and things like that. We eventually got a good team. Every year at Christmas time we used to go to play Redditch on Boxing Day. We had a league, what they call a football combination league. We used to go to them one year and they come to Evesham the next year. Between times, of course, we had other local matches. Badsey were a good team in those days, Badsey Rangers.

Wilfred John Ayres, born 1916

Music

Gentle Entertainment

There used to be quite a few concert parties those days came to Evesham. Men and women, some would sing, soloists or duets, things like that. They used to go round the villages, we had one or two like that with very good voices, one, Victor Newbury was very well known. He was in the church choir as well. And Gertie

Salisbury, she had a dance school and she also ran a concert party for many years. It was a more gentle sort of entertainment we had in those days.

Phyllis Reay, born 1914

Clacking Rib Bones

We had a band at home. We had two rib bones, good big beef rib bones they were that you could clack together and they did make a good noise, I tell you. We used to have a mouth organ, but most of all we used to sing and that was the main thing, and we did sing, I'll tell you!

Olive Thould, born 1918

Buying an Piano Accordion

My father used to play the melodeon and very, very good he was. As a youngster I used to sit on the floor by him and in those days there was no TV, I don't even remember a radio then. Every night it was dad and his melodeon and friends used to come in and there was dancing. One time – this was when I was seven, maybe eight, he looked at me and said, 'Do you want to play?' Of course, I'd never even picked it up. I got hold of it, put it on. I fiddled around for a bit, this was the first time I'd put it on. I proceeded to play all the pieces my dad could play. He looked at me in a way I'd never seen and I was afraid, not realizing he was just simply knocked out because he knew very well that I had never ever touched the thing and there I was playing the pieces he could play. And then I put the accordion down and he picked me up and danced round the room because he thought it was so marvellous. It was nothing to me, but I'd sat and listened to him and I watched him. Then one day my mum took me to some Italian friends and they had a full size piano accordion and she bought it. Must have cost the family fortune then, absolutely – £30, that would be in about 1926, a fortune, £30. Houses, you could buy a house for £75, probably less.

Nick Capaldi, born 1913

Direct From His Continental Engagements

In 1928 my brother, he could play the accordion too, and he'd got an accordion and he was earning his living playing it in the streets, going to Oxford, Swindon, Cheltenham and around the places like that. He was in Swindon one time, he was playing for the theatre queue and he always has somebody going round with a box. A gentleman came up to him and said, 'How would you like to join the show?' He was the manager of the show that was playing there. My brother said to him, 'It's not me you want, it's my young brother', because I was a better player than him, even though I was young. So he came to see my people and frankly, I think it was really one of the worst things that ever happened to me because I should have gone on with my musical training, which would eventually have been much better for me. They fixed up a contract for me to join this show, so it was on May 28 1928 that I joined this revue. They called it a revue in those days, that consisted of a comedian, dancing girls, one or two speciality acts, a leading man, a

Arctic Regions Bazaar, 1914.

leading lady and so on, that was the show. I was met by the manager at the station in Lincoln. He saw me, he came up and said, 'I was told to look for a very small boy with a very large case'. That was me with the accordion you know. So he took me to the theatre and when we got to the theatre, there was a great poster, right across the front of the theatre, in letters that big, you know. '*Nick Capaldi, the wonder boy Italian accordionist, direct from his continental engagements.*' Now the week before I went there I was working for a market gardener here in Evesham, trying to keep the birds off the radishes. That was a job – you had to have long bits of string all along the ground and there were tins tied to it with stones in and you had to keep birds off the plants, you had to keep pulling that string. But the trouble is, the birds got used to noise and it didn't stop them anymore so you had to go running up and down the ground, shouting and screaming, throwing stones and all. That was my continental engagement! I was fourteen and a half.

Nick Capaldi, born 1913

Murder Mysteries at the Pictures

I didn't have many friends because I had my cousins. We used to dash out to Evesham to the pictures. We didn't mind what was on. We used to go on a Saturday morning too. We saw Hopalong Cassidy and Doris Day and Flash Gordon. There were lots of murder mysteries and I loved police films too. We used to play that: we'd pretend we were policewomen and go round the village being nosey and booking down car numbers! It was always a murder mystery thing you were watching and you had two of those,

plus the cartoons and then this other thing with Edgar Lusthaven and the *Pathé News* – and all for about 6d! Your lollipop was only 1d. You'd buy your sweets before you went in, a packet of Spangles, Love hearts, that sort of thing – or fags – those sweet cigarettes.

Sandra Grady, born 1943

The Bug Run

We used to go to see silent films. The pictures was where Somerfield is now. It was a snooker hall when I grew up. The cinema was called the Palace – we used to call it 'the bug run'. Then they opened the Scala, then the Regal. We used to go to the Regal for 9d during the war, 9d, 1s 3d and 1s 6d – all these stairs I used to say, 'They ought to give us 3d to climb these!'

Mrs Doris Greenhalf, born 1913

Jammo James' Peashooter

In Swan Lane, there was a cinema down there, they changed it to a billiards hall after. When it opened it was tuppence to go in and sixpence for the better seats and they were upstairs. You paid to be in the disc [sic], but really it was nearly outside the street! There was orange peel, peashooters, all sorts being thrown about, whilst you were in peril! When you sat in there it was dangerous! The peas from the peashooters would go for miles! And then they used to have a boy, Jammo James we called him, and he was the one that pulled the curtain up. There was a role of clangers [sic] that came down in front of the screen and on the screen there were adverts for all the shops. I distinctly remember Wheatleys shoe shop having an advert at the bottom with two soles of shoes looking at you and when he went down towards the fleapit to pull this thing everybody went 'HURRAY!' So Jammo goes in and pulls up this screen, then they switched on a brilliant blue light. One week you had brilliant blue, the next week you had a brilliant green, the next week yellow or whatever took your fancy and this gave you a colour on the screen and it coloured the picture. I had a headache every time I went, I still went mind, it was worth it. We used to see Walter Miller and Fay Ray in *The Clutching Hand*. Another week you'd have Harry Langdon, *Tramp, tramp*. Before we went in, you went in with a bag of Brighton biscuits from Triangy Lords, which cost about a ha'penny, and chocolate that cost another ha'penny.

Olive Thould, born 1918

Radio and Television

Dick Barton: Special Agent

We had what was called the radio relay. It wasn't in the house, it was transmitted from Cowl Street which is the road that goes off by Woolworths. A man used to be, I suppose, the electrician or the engineer and he got this system that he could turn this radio on and take it to the house. It used to be just a little box on the wall and on the side of this box there used to be a switch and it had got Medium Wave and Luxembourg. It hadn't got FM like they do today. So of course we used to pay sixpence a week so we could have the radio on. We didn't have it till it got going a bit, but then dad decided we could afford it.

I would have been about twelve or thirteen then. It was a great help when we had the radio. Dad used to like to listen to his plays and that, and of course mum used to like the music, well we all liked the music, so we used to have the music. As long as dad could have his serial, quarter to seven till seven, he'd never miss that. It was a detective thing and we all used to have to be terribly quiet when that came on. Father had to listen to his serial – *Dick Barton: Special Agent*, that's what it was called! Used to be good stories to it though, like a cliffhanger, hanging over till the next night making you guess what was going to come.

Dorothy May Sollis, born 1921

Brand New TV

When the TV first came out we had a 9 inch. Harold bought it to see something specially, but I forget what – the Coronation or something like that. It was on wheels and you could push it along, we used to sit glued to the darn thing.

Isabelle Beckley, born 1915

The Coronation on Television

We didn't have a television until 1953, the Coronation, that was our first television. I've never seen our house so full because there wasn't many about! We had lots of visitors in. And it poured with rain, poured and poured for the Coronation. We had one of the barns at the farm and we sat on bales of hay and that's where we had our do at

A Pastoral Play.

night, all the village, at Barrets Farm.

Gladys Davis, born 1911

Dancing

The Hops

If it was a good dance, one of the better ones, it was in the public hall or the town hall, but mostly the public hall. The hops, little dances, the boat people had a wooden hall by the river, opposite the hospital, they used to do teas and let it out for parties and dances and I used to go to those. The scouts and people like that used to have their little hops as they called them.

Phyllis Reay, born 1914

The Walker Hall

The Walker Hall where we'd go when we were kids from the school, they'd have dances there. Refreshments as well, all for a shilling. They used to have the library in there. To heat it they had a big pot bellied stove. Then they took it underground and lit it from below. They're still arguing about it now. It's near derelict. My grandmother told me it was named after Dr Walker who was a parson here for a long time. He paid for it.

Doris Greenhalf, born 1913

The Yanks

It was always a long dress when we went out dancing and black sateen shoes, they used to be 5s a pair. Court shoes, sort of black satin stuff, used to wear those. Used to wear a long dress. 'Run rabbit, run rabbit, run, run, run' was one of the ones we used to dance to. All the modern tunes they'd to play. We had some fun with the Yanks, I can tell you! Me and my friends used to go dancing with them. They were stationed at Aschurch, that's by Tewkesbury and they'd have dances at the camp and we'd to go to the dances and dance with them. They'd always got bags of gum and God knows what else, handing around. They were quite fun, some of them. We had some black Americans as well. They were stationed at Honeybourne. I know one got murdered during the war, a black Yank. He got murdered at Bretforton. That was quite a 'hoo ha'. I don't really know much about it – I just know that someone hit him with a wooden stake or something and it killed him. They used to booze at the pubs there, there were three pubs there, the Fleece and as you go in from Evesham there's one on the left and one on the right, used to be rather, it might be altered now of course.

Isabelle Beckley, born 1915

Lola Taplin

The Fleece is a nice little pub, the landlady was called Lola Taplin. She was a case. We've taken her home many a time from the Golden Hart. She kept a lovely house, you couldn't move the chairs and by the fireplace the rings to keep the witches away. I don't know if she believed in witches, but they were always painted on that fireplace. She had some beautiful pewter. I haven't been there for years of course.

Isabelle Beckley, born 1915

Burnt Through To My Vest

I remember having a pair of dancing shoes. We used to buy either white and have them dyed to match our dress – or black. I bought a pair of gold and green. They were lovely, with pretty buckles on. My mother said, 'You'll regret that my girl. Them heels are too high for you!' I did. I got a nice callus to prove it! The dress was green, in fashion then, they were up in the front and down in the back. Then I had a pretty blue dress with a big bow on the back. The first time I wore it when I got home I said to my mother, 'I've been done!' Somebody had dropped a cigarette down it. Burnt a hole right through to me vest.

Doris Greenhalf, born 1913

Dancing with Teddy

My brothers stayed in Worcester, but they used to come over and of course they thought it was lovely, but the one, the middle one, Teddy, he was a good dancer and as I got a bit older, in my teens, he used to come over and take me to dances. I wasn't allowed to go to dances unless I'd got someone like that with me, but Ted used to come over and take me. That was in the days when they did the Charleston. And he won prizes at it! It was lovely to have a partner like that, because he was quite good looking as well. He had beautiful blond wavy hair.

Phyllis Reay, born 1914

Out and About

Punting

As we got older we more or less lived on the river. We were members of the rowing club for thirty-six years. My husband used to row. I used to like to take a punt out. You could take six in a punt. Three or four of us couples used to hire punts. You had to book them in advance and we used to fill them with cushions and all the food. We used to plan from Sunday to Sunday. We used to go up and over the weir. We'd take two punts over what they used to call the rollers. They were what you pulled the punts up. We used to go from the bottom river to the top river and we used to load up one punt with all the food, and then get into the other. We used to go all the way up to the Fish and Anchor, and go up there to have our lunch, then go further afield. We'd take a ball and a pack of cards and gramophone records and a gramophone. We always had to have a gramophone. Then we'd go on up the river and have our tea … then call at the Boat and we'd fill our two flagons full of water, they filled them for us, then we'd make a fire and boil our water. We'd play about till about four o'clock, then come back down the river, call at the Boat, fill our flagons with cider. This was about sixty or seventy years ago. You could always rely on the weather being nice and we all the same age group. We just took it for granted. We had good times on the river. There again, there was nothing else to do in those days. One of us had a little Morris (car) and one of our friends owned a shop and we'd get all our

The Avon in the 1930s.

Evesham's last barge.

food from them. We'd fill the car with the food we wanted, take it down to the punts and leave the car there till we got back.

Betty Jones, born 1910

Going on the River

We used to have little dances, you know, people used the river more. They'd have these punts on the river, it's not so very deep all around the town, it was quite the thing to go on the river, you'd either have a rowing boat or one of these punts. Bank holidays and days like that in the summer, it used to be absolutely crowded on the river. The regatta used to be a real marvellous day out. They had steam boats, we had ever so many steamers and right through the

summer they used to be very busy. The trains came backwards and forwards and the buses were chocabloc with people coming from Birmingham and that way. It was quite the thing.

Phyllis Reay, born 1914

Clark Hill Covered with Tents

My mother and father lived a little bit further along the town, but it still looked out at Clark's Hill, and bank holidays that used to be covered with tents, the younger people used to come from miles around and bring their tents and stay there for the weekend. I remember the night my daughter was born, it was August bank holiday and I'd been down to the cricket field and back again and I could hear them – they'd to sing at night round the little fires they had by the tents.

Phyllis Reay, born 1914

Playing with George Harrison

George Harrison – you know who he is. I met him at his house. My son, Jim, was very friendly with him. He was in *Traffic*. He said 'Let's go round and see George'. I said, 'That would be great', so we went. As it happened, I'd got a small accordion, it was only a small thing, a student model actually, that people learn with. Jim said 'Let's take that in', he says 'You can play something for George'. Anyway, we took it in and I played this little accordion for him and he was absolutely knocked out. Have a look at that picture and see what it says. 'To Nick. Don't forget your accordion. Call me by 'phone.' You see that 'call me by 'phone' – there's a story there:

Of course, in the '20s, everybody had a ukulele and over the top of sheet music, you can still see it on some sheets of music today, there's little squares on every bar, or it might be every other bar, all according how the harmony changes. And these little squares, you had four strings on the ukulele and they used to put little dots on the strings and that was where you had to put your fingers to produce the correct harmony for that bar, which might be a C Major chord, or an F Major, or a Minor and so on. Everybody got a ukulele, because it was so simple you know. In those days we used to have what they call

Hampton Ferry.

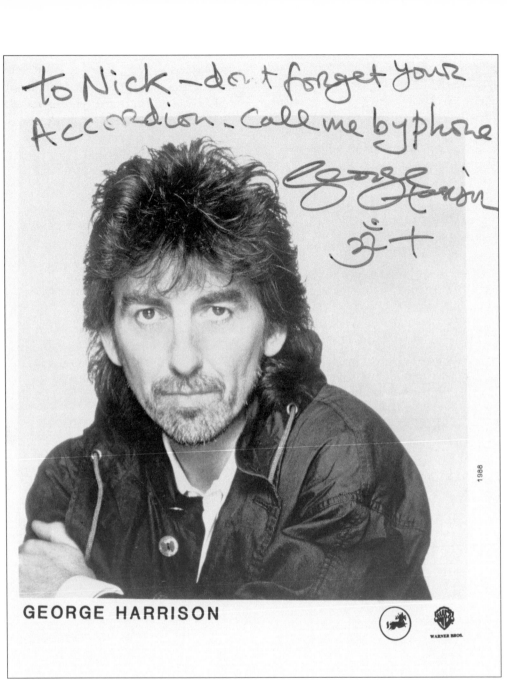

to Nick — don't forget your Accordion — call me by phone

George Harrison

GEORGE HARRISON

1988

WARNER BROS.

Nick Capaldi's signed photograph of George Harrison.

punts on the river, you know what a punt is, a flat boat and they used a big pole. We were always on the river, as often as we could afford, it, we never could afford a punt, my brother and I, we used to have rowing boat, which was cheaper. You'd see somebody going along, people lying back, another with his ukulele sitting facing the people who were relaxing, playing his ukulele and singing. It was up and down the river like that all the time. Anyway George is very interested in ukuleles. 'Anyway,' I said 'in the days when the ukulele first came out, there were no tuners, like you got now, when you play all the notes like what your strings should sound like.' He said 'What did they do?' I said 'well, there were four notes, and they sounded like this -'call me by 'phone' [sung] and that was the four notes. They might not be exactly the key, but if you tuned your ukulele to the way you sang like that, that's how we used to tune our ukuleles.'"And he looked at me. I said, 'You never heard of that?' 'No' he says, 'I'd never heard that. That's a knockout' he says, 'I love it'. So that's why he put it on there.

Nick Capaldi, born 1913

CHAPTER 5

Working Life

Working on the Land

Roasted Cheese

I worked for Bernard and Beryl Ridgewell doing onion tying and parsley picking and sprouts and leeks and bean picking. It was all right in the summer, but I didn't like the winter when you were sprout picking. When it was winter and it was raining you used to have to go up the ground and he'd bring some plastic bags and say, 'Come on, put these on'. You'd put them on your legs and your body and then your coat and hat but I was so short all you could see was my hat bobbing along. I used to get drenched. We'd do marrows in the summer. They were very nice people to work for and we'd have a laugh and we could take the children up and they'd play. He had a stove in the shed and he'd roast a lot of cheese. He'd put cheese on a metal plate and heat it and it would melt then he'd get his bread and dip it in then he'd go back to doing his onions and we'd help to put them on the lorry.

Sandra Grady, born 1943

Paid By Bushel

We still picked in the wet, mind you, you got wet pulling, because you have to pull the string down, you know, then you get the branches off and pick the hops into this crib as they called it … this hessian crib. You pick them in here, you're supposed to get all the leaves out, then a bloke used to come round about twice a day with a big bushel, a proper hop bushel, and he used to bushel them, somebody held the sack at the side and then he used to, so many bushels, and it was booked in a book, then you got your money at the end of the week. You were paid by the bushel. Then in them days, you see, the peas and all that, were picked into pat hampers, you know, proper wicker pat hampers, none of these boxes and such like it is today. I had some happy days there.

Doris Saunders, born 1913

'I Can't Pass That Nora'

I used to tie up, cut cabbage, lettuce, leeks, picked beans, hoe, they used to plant the cabbage thick and then you hoed and singled them out, you know, that was hard, but one of the jobs on the farm was bracing the strings together of the hops. There wasn't many jobs you could do stood up and we had so much an acre, we used to have an acre and you had to tie the strings, two and two, but you had to keep it all level. I remember my brother was foreman and this one woman, because it was a good job when you finished one, if you was lucky you'd get a bit more to do, and she was in such a hurry to get some more that when my brother looked he said, I always remember this, 'I can't pass that Nora'. She said, 'What do you mean?' and he says, 'Well, it's all up and down, up and down, its got to be level' and she was in such a spat she was.

Doris Saunders, born 1913

Dad Was Head Dryer

The string went halfway down to draw the hops together. My dad, he was the head dryer, because they had the kilns up there, and he was the head dryer up there and you know they used to be up there for a week he did, and only come home on a Sunday. Never had their clothes off, just lay and that. Because in them days it wasn't, I mean after it was done by oil and that, but it was like coke and stuff like that and you had to get it to a certain temperature and that. They dried the hops then they put them in pockets, I went up and had a look, and they had a great big iron press and they pressed them and pressed them until the pockets were are hard as that door, really hard before they went off to Worcester, really hard they were. They were used for beer. I loved hop picking. We had like a wooden frame and like a hessian sack over and it closed up and

London House, 1910.

opened out and you had so far in the row, your house as they used, you pulled the hops and picked them off.

Doris Saunders, born 1913

Fruit from the Ministry

I worked for a fruit and vegetable merchant for years, after the war. We served every shop in the town, every canteen, every fish and chip shop, everything. Everybody had it from Sharp's; my area later on was the Cotswolds. I did all the Cotswolds for about twenty-five years, drove myself, a fruit and veg lorry.

See after the war, you didn't sell fruit, it was allocated by the Ministry. One Christmas Eve we had a train load of oranges come into Evesham station – a whole train load – that's where Tesco's is now. We had twenty lorries. It was a big concern, biggest in Evesham – the old ex-service men like. And we came in at four o'clock in the morning and loaded up the oranges, great big wooden cases them days, about hundredweight cases, now they're in little cardboard boxes, but big wooden cases in them days. We delivered them all round, two lorries went round the town here, one lorry went round Pershore and all the villages, another round Bredon and all the villages round there. And two up the hills, one round Bideford on Avon and so on. We served every shop, canteen, hospitals, everything, because you couldn't buy fruit off anybody else, because we were agents for the Ministry, they got to come through Frank Sharp. It was a big, big concern then.

Joe Sherwood, born 1923

Five Acres of Strawberries

We had just five acres of land we rented, just enough to keep us going on our own. Our ground was a long strip $\frac{1}{4}$ mile from top to bottom. We took nearly two ton of strawberries down on little trucks. Cyril pulled it and I pushed at the back and it was

hot! They used to have to be picked and then they were put on the train at Evesham – the four o'clock train, the fruit train and it went to Manchester and all over the place.

Gladys Davis, born 1911

Picking Plums

I did hop pick when I was a little kid like. My mother used to go hop picking, pea picking, bean picking, but I didn't like hop picking much. Used to make you tired. Plum picking's hard work – up and down the ladder all the time, especially if it's a bit wet, the ladder kept sticking in the mud, walking up and down with a big basket on your side

Asparagus Sale, Smithfield, 1912.

67

full of plums and it used to cut into your side. Them days, you got to pick 12lbs of plums for 6d. If they were for jam they used to pick them in big wooden square crates and that was only 1s 6d a crate for jamming plums. If they were little plums that you were jamming it would take you three or four hours to get anything near the full. Didn't earn much at that.

Bernard Hunt, born 1922

Get Up or I'll Knock You Down

You'd see the same people every year coming, same lot. They used to all come from Birmingham and Dudley, because they had big barracks like at Wick, they stopped in these barracks these Brummies did and Friday and Saturday nights they used to go to Pershore and get three parts drunk and they used to come back along the village shouting and singing and dad would say, 'Did you hear them last night?' he'd say, 'they was fighting – I heard one bloke say "get up or I'll knock you down"'. Well how could he do that if he was already down?

Bernard Hunt, born 1922

What About My Washing?

The Dudley people used to come down from Birmingham on the train to pick the

Coulters Garage, c. 1935.

raspberries, they used to pick them in buckets and dad used to weigh these little round tubs and chalk the side the weight of the tub. Then they used to tip the raspberries into the tubs and that's how they did it. It was a very big farm. The women, my mum, they used to tie all the new canes in the winter with a little ball of string, then they used to come down for hop picking again. The farm there, they had their own railway line and trucks up to the Fladbury station and my mum used to go to work on a Saturday morning and she used to say to Captain Bomford, 'Well what about my washing?' and he said, 'You can turn Phil Pott's shirt and put it on again'.

Doris Saunders, born 1913

Captain Bomford

Captain Bomford was a bit of a genius, he was thirty years ahead of his time in always inventing new methods, new machinery and new ways of doing things not only with regards to ground working machinery but with hop picking systems and also with the livestock. He built the first hop machine that was ever made. It worked a treat and everybody from all over the Worcestershire hop fields and even down from Kent used to come and copy and have a model for their own. After that they also, twice a year, had what you used to call an open day and it used to last for two or three days, people from all over the world, Europe, Canada and America used to come and see all his latest methods for market gardening.

When I was with Captain Bomford I did all kinds of tractor driving. They had one big tractor with a hydraulic system on the back and we did the hoe cropping work vegetables and potatoes everything and helped with the

harvesting and in those days a binder behind the tractor. In those days the tractors did not have batteries but you had to crank them up by hand. The old system was that you had a thin grade of oil in the winter and a thick grade in the summer. We used to have to change it about once a month in the winter, when it was freezing. The only way you could start the tractor was to get a thing like a big long rod that had a handle on the end and put some diesel fuel on it, light it and open the manifold plate on the side and you would turn it and it would draw the fire in as you turned it to start up the diesel.

Bill Atkinson, born 1921

Riddling the Potatoes

In them days I can remember my mum riddling potatoes down the dry in the winter. They buried the potatoes in them days in great big long buries and covered them with dirt and then they used to get them out and they had to be riddled on an old riddle – you know and sorted and bagged and that, and they used to wear what we called a 'urden apron' (an apron made of sort of sacking). The potatoes were buried because of the frost. They had straw over them you see – great big long buries they had at the end of the row with the potatoes when I left. My birthday's the 5 October and I left at the end of October because it was half term and my mum was picking up potatoes then so I done it for a couple of weeks until I got a job. Mum had 5d an hour and I had 2d halfpenny. The tractor used to go round and round, digging 'em out and I used to pick my length up and half mum's.

Doris Saunders, born 1913

Steamers on the Avon.

The Man from the Ministry

Years ago, there was a bloke called S.J. Grove, Sammy Grove, and he always had about four or five steamers there, and punts and boats and all down the river, it was a busy place then. He got down to one steamer and he sold that to a bloke called Tolley, so – this is a laugh, this is – so he converted it from steam to diesel, but he got to get the Weights and Measures bloke from the Ministry to reweigh the thing for the weights. So they got no weights, so they rang up our firm and asked if they could borrow a load of potatoes. So I went down there with a great big Leyland lorry with 11 ton of spuds on in hundredweight, they was hundredweights in those days and we had to put two on each seat to represent people to weigh it. We had to carry them down, the best bit was, we get them down, two of us, who pulls up in this great big wagon load of

spuds, and Tolley said to us 'You've got to find the Inspector from the Ministry'. I says, 'Where from?' and he says, 'Cheltenham station'. 'Well,' I says, 'I ain't taking this ruddy great load of spuds to Cheltenham'. 'Oh', he says, 'borrow my car'. So Des Evans, who was a mate of mine, says, 'Hey, you drive it, Joe, I don't drive these posh cars'. I said, 'Hey, what's the bloke look like?' 'Oh', he says, 'You can't mistake him, he'll have a bowler hat on, a rolled umbrella, and a briefcase'. So we gets into Lansdowne station at Cheltenham, because I knew me way around, and I pulls in there and the train come in and about 200 people get off that train, and they all got bowler hats, rolled umbrellas and briefcases! So Des looks at me and says, 'What do we do now, Joe?' I says, 'Wait a minute, Des, wait until they've thinned out a bit, and if we see an old boy who's lost on his own, I'll go up and tackle him'. He said, 'You go, I ain't going'.

So I picked on the right bloke, he was Ministry. I says, 'I'm from Mr Tolley of Evesham' so I brought him back. We had to carry all these spuds, about two hundredweight of spuds on each seat, to represent people for him to weigh the boat. Then we had to move from one side of the boat to the other, and we nearly turned the blinking boat over, because of the weight, then we had to pick them all up, carry them on our shoulders and re-stack them on the lorry. We took them to Pershore market and unloaded the damn lot again. He gave us 10s and a case of beer, about twenty tins of beer, and we earned it, I'll tell you.

Our picture was in the paper, we had, it was the *Evesham Journal*, it was the *Evesham Standard* in them days, and me and my mate's picture and the lorry and everybody was stood on the old bridge at Evesham, saying 'Mr Sharp's sending his spuds by boat now', they didn't know we was only putting them on there for weights for the boat. It was quite a laugh that day. It was hard work though. It was hard work in the fruit trade them days, everything was heavy, see, there was no fork lifts and pallets in them days, everything was man-handled.

Joe Sherwood, born 1923

Waking Early

I was working on the land. I wasn't actually called into the Land Army, but I worked on the land like a Land Girl was. And I know in the summertime when the asparagus cutting was and we used to be down the ground at five o'clock in the morning and soon as we'd cut it we had to start and go round again. We was doing this about three

Land army girls and local men. Bill Heritage (Ethel Marion's husband) is second from the left, middle row.

An agricultural worker and his contraption.

times a day. Many a time when he's [my boyfriends] come to meet me, he's found me down there. 'Come on' he says, 'It's your night off'. My mother didn't use to like it really, but he put a stop to that. 'No, you does enough hours in the daytime, and that's it'. I know I done sprout picking and all. We used to have a pair of boots on and when the wellingtons wore out at the bottom, we used to cut the tops off and slide them up our legs before we put our boots on and used to go sprout picking that way. It was all on coupons those days, so it was a bit of hard time. We still wake early in the morning now. It's a habit we got into.

Florence Edna Elizabeth Hunt, born 1927

Growing Asparagus

It's too expensive to grow asparagus these days. You only get the one crop in twelve months and you've got about three lots of labour. You've got to dig the beds all out, takes two or three weeks to do. You have to pay all the staff to do that, then there's the fertiliser to put on and then after that you've got to rake it all down in the spring down to fine soil before it grows through. There's a lot of work and expense put into it but you've only got the one crop and if it doesn't come a good crop, you've lost. Still it always was a gamble, market gardening, back as far I can remember.

Bernard Hunt, born 1922

Market Gardening

My father had land; he had land produce you know, he did vegetables and all that. My brother still does it, he's still got the land, my dad's land, he's eighty yet he still does it – out behind Hinton. He lives there. Asparagus was the main thing, it's lovely isn't it, we had some every weekend. We'd treat ourselves every week. He used to grow that and it was very cheap, now it's very dear. He used to sell it at Evesham market. Whether the market's there or not now, the job itself has gone. Market gardening gone. It's all coming in from abroad now. I don't think much of it and they're not giving this GM food a good name are they. They reckon we've got to be careful. We don't know what to have; I read the other night you have to be careful. We buy a lot of organic; it's the best of the two.

Ethel Marion Heritage, born 1913

Ethel Marion Heritage in service at eighteen years old in 1931.

Ethel Marion Heritage at Abersock in 1931.

Careful What You Do

We never used to wonder if it was safe to eat this and eat that. I used to cook sprouts and potatoes, but we'd never heard of organic food – it's a new word with me. I expect it had got a different word. Everything now seems to be trumped up, twisted round, but I don't remember having to be afraid of doing this and afraid of doing that, we've got to be careful what we do all the time now.

Ethel Marion Heritage, born 1913

In Service

In Service with the Highmans

My auntie come down from a big house near Windsor and she was a ladies maid and my uncle, she was mum's sister, he was a butler. She said 'Oh Doris, I'd like you to come back with us', so I went back up there to work. I was a little old fashioned maid in a black dress and white apron and cap. These people was diamond merchants and it was a huge place, fifteen in staff, two chauffeurs and three gardeners and this was their weekend house. And one of the sons was to do with films and we used to have Cecily Courtenage and Jack Hulbert and all down there at the weekends. Mrs Highman said to my auntie 'Oh Helen, for goodness sake, buy Doris some different clothes, she looks so old'. And I remember my auntie made me some pretty morning dresses and I always remember she made me an afternoon dress and it was long waist and I thought I was the cats whiskers. It was a very pretty blue, a long bodice with box pleats around the bottom; it was really nice. Mrs Highman used to ring the bell and I used to go up in the bathroom, you can imagine it was all pink marble and this scent in big decanters on the side. It was marvellous. She used to have me up there and she used to give half a crown each for us. Mind you that was a lot of money in them days.

It was an eye opener to me, being in London, because the sheets on the lady's bed was all crepe de chine and big monograms in the middle and had to have a clean nightie on every day. There was two daughters and they used to go to Ascot like every year and every day they all had different dresses on and I used to help auntie to dress them and get them ready and there were these great big long wardrobes in her bedroom all full of Norman Hartnell and them dresses and diamonds. She had about that width of diamonds on her arm, and them girls, you know. They used to use this big house, it had got a tower and all, more as a weekend house, but she used to go backwards and forwards to London, in a Buick car with all these jewels in a case. Well, they wouldn't do it today, would they? No way, no way. Sir Michael Balkan, I've seen his name on the telly, he married Mrs Highman's niece. He used to come there to meals. We used to have a lot of film stars there to weekend parties like.

Well you can imagine, a little country girl that had never been anywhere or done anything, only you know, in this area, to go up to a place like that, well it was a different world, I used to go up to London to help up there at the town house sometimes. When I was at Hendon we used to have Sunday morning and half a day, and taken the next week you had Sunday afternoon and one half a day, but you had to get everything done.

But I left Hendon Hall because this old cook shopped me, but she was carrying on with the gardener, soon as Mrs Farncombe went from the door, she was up in the potting shed with the gardener. Anyhow, I told her, shopping me because Den comes and speaks to me, I said, 'little do you know when your cars gone, she's up in the potting shed with the gardener'.

Doris Saunders, born 1913

Serving Neville Chamberlain

I had to go into domestic service. That was it then, we didn't have the choice of nice jobs like they do today. We had to say Master and Mistress and Sir and Madam, wear caps and aprons and behave ourselves,

Bournemouth, 1933. Ethel Marion Heritage (left) on holiday while working with the Greys.

Bournemouth, 1933. Ethel Marion Heritage (left) on holiday while working with the Greys.

Port Street, c. 1920.

remember who we were. I worked for Neville Chamberlain, the War Minister, Prime Minister. That was in 1927 and I worked there for three years, then I moved about. I wanted a change. I wanted to move about. I worked my way up to be cook because that was the posh job. I was twenty-one or twenty-two. I started off as housemaid making the beds, doing the bedrooms and then I was parlour maid, the dining room, silver cleaning and all that. Then we had dinner parties. We had to fold the napkins for every meal – linen napkins. Every meal we had to fiddle like this and do water lilies, mitres, slippers and so on – it was fiddly because and we could have done it so much quicker if it hadn't been for this wretched folding the napkins.

Ethel Marion Heritage, born 1913

Laying Up Properly

We had to lay properly, the nearer the meal the further away. Knife fork, knife fork, pudding, the earlier the meal the farther away you took, the last course was inside. But, oh dear, they wouldn't do it today. My daughter says she wouldn't do it, but I loved it. They (the Greys) used to take us away on holiday with them, but we only had to do the minimum of work. We didn't have to do all this fiddle faddle as I call it – we only had to … so we could get out a bit. We didn't go out of this country, Wales was the farthest – I went to Abersock, Caernarfon, we had the chauffeur to take us about. The sooner we did our work, the sooner we got out.

Ethel Marion Heritage, born 1913

Holidays with the Family

They made it our holiday, to a point, which was very nice because mother was very short and the '30s was the worst decade of all. There were four maids as a rule and they used to save their money up to go to Holland, £7 for a week and it took them saving. We got about 15s a week, we got our food as well, but we had to buy clothes. These other girls said, 'Couldn't you manage to come with us to Holland and Belgium?' No – well my money wasn't as much as theirs, not what I'm talking now – I was quite young, a teenager and I couldn't manage it. It was only £7, but it was a heck of a lot of money.

The holidays lasted a month, because they wanted a month and of course we had a month as well because they wanted it didn't they? They couldn't do any work, they weren't trained to work and as long as they were there, we got to be there, but as I say, it was the minimum of work. The daughters used to do some of it so we could get out, they did help us a lot. They were nice people.

Ethel Marion Heritage, born 1913

Hated Service

I left school at fourteen then I was bunged in service. It was horrible! I hated it! I used to have to get up in the morning and clean the range, blacklead it, light the fire, make tea for the old cook, and then I used to have to lay the table for the servants to have their breakfast. I didn't stick that for very long, I can tell you.

Isabelle Beckley, born 1915

Working at the Confectionery

At fourteen of course, I went into service down at Vine Street. It was a confectionery, they sold everything, you know: rock and cigarettes and sweets for the tourists. Behind that was a man's barber shop and behind that was the house and they had two children. Well, I was only fourteen, but I used to have to get up at six in the morning and go to bed at ten o'clock at night, because I used to have to do all the cooking. I used to have to do all the washing. I used to have to look after the two young boys because the mother and the Granny looked after the shop, the daughter's husband ran the man's barber shop and of course it left me to do it all, the washing, cooking … everything. I had 4 shilling a week, but I used to give my mother a shilling, even though I wasn't at home, but of course I used to have to clothe myself and that was a lot in those days.

Dorothy May Sollis, born 1921

Other Work

Apprentice to a Milliner

I think I was nearly fifteen when my mother saw the sign to be an apprentice from the millinery and I thought I'd like that, because I'd always liked sewing and we made hats in those days. I also picked up dressmaking because they had a dressmaker there and when we were quiet in the millinery I used to have to go and help her. So I learnt quite a few useful tips there. I did dressmaking after I was married for quite a long time.

I earned 2s 6d, half a crown a week –

that'd be 12 pence now! I had that for two years, and then I went up to 5 shillings. You start off really right from the bottom and you have to sweep the floor, clean the floor, pick up the pins and make sure everything was all clean – I used to do that first thing in the morning. And then I had to watch the actual milliner when she did things. We were taught to put linings in hats, that's another thing you don't see now, I don't suppose you could buy a hat lining and you had a special stitch for that. Then we were shown how to trim a hat, how to make a bow, there were special stitches for that. Then sometimes if someone wanted a hat, but it was a bit big, there was a special way of making the lining smaller so that the hat fitted better. And of course you did all the running about if they wanting anything fetching, until you went up a grade. You started right at the bottom, but I did pick up a lot of useful things. For a long time after I left, people used to bring their hats to me to trim. There was one dear old lady, who lived up Bengeworth, and she used to wear one of these bonnets that ties under the chin and she used to bring her bonnet in every spring, summer and autumn to be re-trimmed for whatever was suitable for the time of year. It was ever so sweet. It used to be flowers in the summer, feathers in the winter and sometimes the ribbons wanted to be renewed and you big broad ribbons to tie under the chin with a big bow – I used to love doing that, trimming these bonnets.

I also was taught to make these things they used to wear when they working in the fields. They used to wear these bonnet things, with a piece at the back of the neck to keep the sun off. It was made with material, something like linen and you pleated it and sewed it which made it a bit firm and then there was piece at the back to keep the sun off. Very sensible things really. And of course they would have big aprons.

Phyllis Reay, born 1914

Fastest Driver

Most of the fruit and veg came from locally; we went up to Covent Garden Market twice a week, in London. I went down there Mondays and Wednesdays, in the old market, when it was just off Trafalgar Square. You got to go leave here at midnight to get a place to park your lorry, because it was chockablock. They had to move it in the finish. It's at Nine Elms now, see, by

E.H. Summers, the Bakers Cart.

79

Vauxhall Bridge. But those days, because we had an agent down there. We got there about three in the morning and we had to sleep in the cab till the market opened at half past five, just to park your lorry and get back here in the evening. And in the summer, when the plums were around, we served plums all over the country, in the '50s. We went to Boston, Peterborough, all around the canning factories, Liverpool, Manchester, London, all over the place and to Leeds. We'd knock off work at ten and get back in the lorries at midnight and drive up to Leeds. Lorries them days was hard work, there was no motorways. We used to leave at midnight here with a load of plums on for Leeds, Moorhouses jam factory in Leeds, to get there for seven. It took us seven hours to get up there. We used to have 560 boxes of plums on the back for canning, golden plums they used to call them. We went to Boston, to the United Canners at Boston, and Louth, we went to Farrers of Peterborough, Chivers at Istan, Hartleys at Liverpool, oh, Dewers Jams at Manchester, we went all over. The farthest we went was Robertson's, the main factory was in Bristol, they got one in Nuneaton, they got one Charlesdon in Manchester and they got one in Manchester, Paisley. Oh, it was a long ride from here to Paisley. It took us three days. To get up there and back. We had Leylands and Pettigrews. They were big. There was no power steering in them days or air brakes. We had a thing on, I was driving for 59 hours and I got pinched once for speeding. And I was doing 47 mile an hour, out in the open country – 47 – I was restricted to 30 mile an hour. And then when I got pulled up at Congleton, when I got back to Stafford to see a Frank Sharp lorry in a lay-by, my old mate. I pulled in behind him. I said, 'What's the matter, Vic?

Don't look so bloody happy'. He says, 'I've just been done for log books'. We had to carry log books them days, no tachometers. 'Copper said I was the fastest driver he'd ever known', according to my log book I went to Evesham to Wolverhampton in 2 minutes. I got £5 quid fine and my licence endorsed for speeding.

Joe Sherwood, born 1923

The Man From Brum

It's a rich place round here. Because it was all big market gardeners, all the, men you touched your cap to. When you met old Frank Sharp, you called him sir and he didn't call you by your Christian name, it was 'Brown!' 'Smith!' Them days. And they used a lot, see it was grown for asparagus, it was known for asparagus, Evesham. And the vegetables, but a lot of merchants round here used to hire fields off the people in the Cotswolds, round Snowshill, Broadway, those hills, to grow the sprouts you see, they had sheep on the fields all the year, then they'd plough em all up and plant all sprouts. They used to make a mint. They used to run busloads of people round here to pick the sprouts. We had two auction markets those days, in Evesham, Smithfield at the top, by the station, which is all houses now, and there was the central market and they used to auction 'em. Have you ever been to an auction market with veg? It's quite an education. It's out at Often now, you know, little growers bring all little bits of produce and they puts it down, then the auctioneer comes round and 'Come on, lads' and they rattle away, these auctioneers, you know. These merchants, they used to come from miles around, all round the Midlands to buy their veg from Evesham. Used to have one old boy, come from Brum, and he come down and he'd buy about thirty crates of cabbage, off the market, and he always came to our place and we did a pre-packing plant, and all the rejects he bought, cheap. They were 5s a bag and he went to Birmingham and he'd peel em, chip em and go round the hotels. And he made a living at it. Cabbages and all things like that. Quite an education that is. But this fruit market, don't shout or anything, or you'll buy it. This one, at about half ten, eleven o'clock everyday and all the veg is laid out, and they auction it.

Joe Sherwood, born 1923

Home & Colonial

I was delivering groceries in the grocery trade. In those days any large orders like that were delivered by an errand boy. Today of course with the cars about now, so many cars they usually want to take their groceries home themselves, but I delivered the orders on a bicycle with a basket on the front. This was in Evesham. It was a small shop, Drew Alley they call it now I think, it's a sort of pathway or roadway between Bridge Street and High Street and we were along there. There was also the Maypole, they were part of the same syndicate. We were called the Home & Colonial tea stores, we specialized in dry goods, in tea and coffee and whatnot. The Maypole was called the Maypole Dairy and were on dairy products like cheese and butter. Well, we were all supplied by Allied Suppliers, same firm, all belonged to the Allied Suppliers. They had their butter from the Allied Suppliers, the Home & Colonial had their butter from Allied Suppliers and

customers would come to me in the shop. There were no pre-packed stores in those days, you had to weigh it all yourself and some people would come in and you'd ask them if they wanted butter, 'Oh no, we always get our butter from the Maypole'. So I'd say we have the same sort of butter, but they weren't impressed, they would have to go to the Maypole to get their butter.

Wilfred John Ayres, born 1916

Work a Willing Horse

We moved into Bridge Street and we were next door to the Maypole and I was then a boy at the time and when I delivered the groceries and I came back, very often I went into the Maypole thinking it was the Home & Colonial, because it was next door to one another. We lived in a flat above the tobacconists in Bridge Street and we were in the rooms above this shop. I went back for twelve months after the war and rationing was still on. Anyway, there was no scope at all then. At that time they still only had what they were rationed, there was no salesmanship or anything. The wages were very low. I think when I was first hand there, that was under manager, I was only getting about 10s a week and prices were sky high elsewhere and we had no union on those days to get you more money, so you had to ask for yourself. But if you asked for a rise, invariably they'd say we can't afford it or something, unless it was very urgent and I was told the next time you want a rise, tell them you've got another job. Which I hadn't, but I was going to leave and go to another job with more money. So they sent the inspector down, they had inspectors

Evesham Journal *staff*, c. 1950.

come down about every month to check on everything and they said, 'Why are you leaving?' and I said, 'Well, I can't afford to live on what I'm getting'. 'If you could get more money, would you stay on?' I was eager to say yes, but I didn't give them a definite answer, so they said, 'where do you live?', and I said only just down the road. He said, 'Well go down the road and see your mother and ask her whether you should stay on here' and course it was already determined that I was going to stay on in any case. I think I had about 10s extra a week – quite a lot in those days and if I hadn't said I was leaving they wouldn't have bothered. It's very true what they say – work a willing horse.

Wilfred John Ayres, born 1916

He Loved His 'Hosses'

My dad took up this job as a groom because he was always very keen on horses, and we went to live at a place called Overbury and it was a tied cottage there, but they both died in the cottage, they were there years and years. He looked after hunters and some used to have foals and he used to go and foal them. He loved his 'hosses'. He had quite a few hunters because he worked for Holland Martins and they had sons that used to go hunting and they used to race at Cheltenham races, used to take one or two of their horses to the races. I was frightened of horses. My father was most disappointed because I didn't like horses. No, I was frightened of them. My sisters didn't ride, but I don't think they were as frightened as me. I was terrified of the damn things.

Isabelle Beckley, born 1915

Telephone Line Fitter

I did enjoy my work and never had a Saturday off in my life you see, Saturday was always a busy day in the grocery trade. It was very late hours. We started at eight or half past in the morning, dinnertime we'd have an hour, back again at two o'clock and then you go on then until about five. Sometimes you'd stop for tea, other times you'd carry on working until seven or eight o'clock at night, particularly at the beginning of the week when everything had to be weighed up. One day in the week you were only told to finish by 1.30 midday. That was one day in the week, that was by law and that of course was the only half day you got.

But when I came out of the army, I wanted to continue in this communications business so I wrote to the telephone manager asking for an interview to see if they could find a job for me in telecommunications. Well, I went. Well he told me at least that there were no vacancies on the engineering side but would I take a job as a postman. Well, if I knew then what I know now I would have taken that job because I could have transferred onto the engineering side and I would have had extra years on my pension. But as I say I didn't know at the time and it wasn't until much later that I was told that it wasn't the telephone manager but the general manager in Birmingham you want to see. So I wrote to him and within a short time they sent back to say I was to go for an interview for being offered a job. Well I went on the interview and told them what my qualifications were and that I was keen to get onto the communications side and that's when I started. It wasn't long before I was on telephones. I started as a linesman, putting up poles and whatnot. Started at the bottom and that went on for about two years I should think and in that time I progressed to be a telephone fitter, just a simple fitter that when the lines were laid I went and put a 'phone on the end – nothing technical about it. That's where I started. As I progressed I went on various courses, again communications subjects, switchboards, in-house exchange systems and things like that and eventually I was a full-grown fitter. I didn't do putting up poles then; I still had to climb poles to connect wires up to the poles. Eventually I was fitting switchboards and that would be a good job because the cables you use for that. In one cable alone you probably have two pairs of wires to each telephone. Of course people just think it's a simple thing to fit a telephone on the end, but sometimes I had to fit an extension in the bedroom or whatnot and then of course I had to alter the cables in the telephone to make it work. Because if you just teed the line in together, had the two on the same line, when you dialled out from one telephone it would tinkle the bell on the other, so you had a lot of connections in the telephone to stop that.

Wilfred John Ayres, born 1916

Cleaning up for the Ball

January – always the busiest month of the year January was. Well, in January, when we had parties, we used to have dinner in the town hall and a ball in the public hall and you used to have to go across from the town hall to this ball to five o'clock in the morning when the licensees used to take all their bottles and stuff out of the building, and we had to start work again at seven o'clock in the morning so we didn't go to bed. And we used to have to change, have our breakfast and go back to work at seven o'clock. I was going over and helping Mr Turner clear up and sweeping up and in those days, after a ball or a dinner. You used to start at one end of the hall with brooms in a row, three of us, with wetted tea leaves, and then they used to put powder down on the floor to make it slippery ready for dancing again. But if we'd had a dinner, that's what we used to have to do, put the powder down, you know, ready for balls. A dinner one day, or a concert and you got to put chairs in that, they were three seaters in those days, fold up three seaters and you got to lift them up and pack them in one room ready for clearing the room for something else. Oh God, it was hard work.

And, I'll tell you what, I had 13s 4d a week off the Council, the four years, I was married in 1926, till I had my baby in 1930. And Able & Smiths were putting the electric in and the decorators came from Brierley Hill and these men used to lodge up Port Street lodgings and they used to be dressed up in navy blue suits to go to the Plough on the corner. The town hall for their drink at night and they'd see the light on the public hall and they'd come and in and they'd say, 'hey – come on out of it, you've been here since seven o'clock this morning and its time you finished. We'll put the lights out if you don't. So come on and lock that door'. And I'd been scrubbing all day and I had to carry this big galvanized bucket from the basement, soda water, me scrubbing brush, a piece of soft soap and my

floor cloth and carry it all up right up into the gallery and I scrubbed all those rooms and the ballroom floor, all the library, all down, it's the precinct now where everybody walks. I've scrubbed all that, right down in the basement where they used to have the bar and the cooking when we cooked for 400. I've known about work in my day!

Catherine Maude Turner, born 1902

84

CHAPTER 6

Wartime

Abbey Manor Red Cross Hospital.

Women Working

The Waybill

I heard Chamberlain on the radio one Sunday morning – I'll always remember it and we listened to his speech on the radio. He said he'd been waiting for a piece of paper to come from Hitler to say that he wouldn't invade somebody, but he said 'I have to tell you now, there is no piece of paper, so we are at war with Germany' and we expected aeroplanes to come over the next minute and bomb us, but they didn't come of course.

My father had already been through one war, but he went in the Home Guard, he was very good. I wasn't frightened, I forget what I was doing – oh, I was working at the laundry. I thought I'd better do something and I worked on the buses, I did. I was a bus conductress. I loved it. We had a uniform and stacks of tickets and what have you. I used to go from Evesham to Gloucester twice a day, morning and afternoon. The fare used to be 2s return, I bet it's more than that now. We had a little ticket machine where you pressed it in and it went 'ting' and a thing which we called a waybill. When you started on your duty, you had to put the numbers of the tickets, the first numbers of the tickets on your rack on this waybill, when you finished you had to put the finishing numbers then you had to subtract and had to balance your money up. It had to be right, I'll tell you. If it was wrong you had to put it in out of your own pocket, so you were always very careful with change, at least I tried to be. Made a mistake sometimes, we all do don't we?

Isabelle Beckley, born 1915

I Chose the Factory

I was living in Barnt Green during the war, not long, a very few months, then I had my call up papers and I had to go in either the forces or the factory and I chose the factory. There was a factory right near where my mother lived and I thought it was handy to keep an eye on her. I chose the factory. It was packing food for the soldiers on the front. They wanted to eat, didn't they? The factory was Toddington, near Winchcombe, between here and Cheltenham.

Ethel Marion Heritage, born 1913

Sick Note to See My Husband

I worked on ammunitions for a time at Worcester. It was to make bullets. It was Cadbury's factory – you know Cadbury's chocolate? They had a factory at Worcester, so when it really got started, the government took it over, they had all the places like that for munitions and we made bullets and we had to do shift work. And we could not get a day off. You had to be practically on your deathbed to have a day off. If you had a day off it was terrible. You were called to the office the next morning and severely reprimanded. Well, I was married when I worked there and if my husband was coming home on leave, I used to go to my doctor, he used to look at me when I walked in and say 'Hello Dorothy, husband coming home, is he?' That was before I said a word! I said 'Yes' and he'd write me a prescription out. And that's true, I had to get a doctor's prescription to get a few days with my husband when he come home on leave. It's unbelievable what went on in the war.

Dorothy May Sollis, born 1921

Hospital Work in the Wars

I worked ten years at Evesham Cottage Hospital. The second time I went I was there five years. They trained me in the First World War and then I went back in the Second World War when I was married. That's the second matron I worked for – Matron Tyrell. There's a row of houses, where the hospital stood, its called Tyrell Terrace and that was her name. It's named after her. She was in the First World War you see, but I worked for her in the Second World War when she was at Evesham hospital.

Catherine Maude Turner, born 1902

Hospital staff outside Abbey Manor.

Another picture of hospital staff outside Abbey Manor.

Battered Jam Sandwiches

I was working at the nurses' home, it's flats now, that's still there in Briar Close. I tell you what I used to have to do for the nurses, you know a double saucepan, like a porridge saucepan, you have water in the bottom and whatever you want to cook you have it in the top. Well I had to boil rice in a double saucepan, cook it until it was absolutely soft, and then I used to put pepper and salt and egg powder and margarine or butter or whatever mix it all thoroughly, do rounds of toast and that, during the war, was scrambled egg. And I did it for all, matron and all. Another thing, during the Second World War, I was helping in the cooking line; we used to go on duty on Monday and on Sunday. They had everything cold, the troops, whatever they had, jam sandwiches, all different, all cold. Well all these jam sandwiches which were left on Monday we used to dip into a batter and brown them each side and sell them to the soldiers for, I don't know if it was 3d or 6d and they used to come and they were marvellous, they thought they were beautiful. And it was only jam sandwiches, done in the batter, browned and you know, so there's all those funny things you did during those times you know and there was lots of things that we used to make do and mend sort of thing.

Catherine Maude Turner, born 1902

BBC in Evesham

During the war, I worked at the BBC, because they brought the BBC down to Evesham from London. Everything come down to Evesham, it was the main headquarters. We had all the foreign monitors, as they was called, that give all the foreign news out. We had the orchestras, the Midland orchestra, all the orchestras, all the news readers, and a lot of them was billeted in Evesham. I worked in the canteen. I dished the food out, they'd come in and order something and I'd give it to them.

Dorothy May Sollis, born 1921

A Beautiful Piano

Actually, there were four of us worked there [at the BBC during the war], my dad, my brother, my sister and I worked. So of

Outside Abbey Manor.

The Engineering Training Department at Wood Norton Hall.

course, they was all Londoners that worked there and we got friendly with them, we used to take them home and have a good sing song, especially some of them that we knew that were in the orchestra. And there was one, his name was Donald Edge and he used to come because he knew the girls from London, the one was the supervisor of the canteen, so he'd go and have a drink with them sometimes. She said, 'I'm going to bring Donald up to your house one day to play your piano because it's a beautiful piano, its got a beautiful sound, I think he'll like it'. Anyway she decided to bring two or three or them up one day. She said, 'This is Donald, he's in the Midland orchestra and he wants to play your piano'. Mother was there and I said, 'Well he won't beat mother, she plays the best'. He says to her, 'We'll have a competition then, mother'. So mother laughed and she said. 'Carry on, you know. If you want to play, play'. He played

and he said, 'I've never played such a beautiful piano in all my years. It's even better than the one I play in the orchestra'. It was a beautiful piano, it was the tone you see. He was really thrilled.

Dorothy May Sollis, born 1921

D-Day on the Buses

Doing shiftwork was terrible. The buses still ran, I mean they didn't have much light to see where they were going, they had to cover the lights half over, just a glimmer. We used to go eight in the morning till five and then we used to go six at night till eight the next morning. I can always remember, I was working there on D-Day, it stands out in my memory, because all the planes went over here. The sky was black with planes going to France from all the aerodromes around this way. I was waiting for the bus to take me to work and we didn't know what was going on – they didn't give it out that they was going to Dunkirk to start the end of the war as you might say. They couldn't give it out on the radio. I saw all these planes and I thought, 'Whatever's going on?' We used to see one or two go over occasionally, but not that many, there were dozens of them.

Dorothy May Sollis, born 1921

Away at War

First Class Home Guard

When I was with the Bomfords, in 1938, I went to Hull which was a big seaport, but I had to have two perfect eyes to go on the ships. But that didn't stop me being in the home guard. I joined the force in Worcestershire and sometimes we used to go

on exercise in Tydesley Wood with the airforce. We used to have tests and things for everything even with the gun. When I went to all these tests, battle and field work the only thing I never did was the anti tank gun because two special men were doing that. Everything else I passed and what they gave you was a little red triangle under a bronze strip – a proficiency badge – and I was the only one in Hampton that had one. They were a good first class home guard, they had to go and guard the power station and places like that, so I went through the war and did my bit.

Bill Atkinson, born 1921

Calling up Artistes

I was called up of course for World War II. The story behind that is we had an invitation to go to Drury Lane Theatre to do an audition for ENSA (Entertainment for the

The Worcesters going into action.

maj S B Carter m.B.E.

4th Worcestershire (Evesham) Battalion Home Guard

You are invited to attend

A DINNER

of the Officers of the Battalion which will be held at Wood Norton (by kind permission) on Saturday, 18th November, 1944, at 7.30 for 8 p.m.

Dress: Uniform or Morning Dress
R.S.V.P. to your Company Commander
or to Capt. H. Woods, Wick House, Pershore

An invitation to the Officer's mess dinner at Wood Norton, 1944.

MENU	TOASTS
❦	Toast Master: Major G. C. Lees-Milne
	❦
Mock Turtle Soup	
————	The King Mess President: Maj. G. C. Lees-Milne
Roast Chicken	Vice-President: Lt. M. J. Hodges
Roast Goose	
————	The Battalion Major R. H. Stallard, M.C.
Baked Potatoes Creamed Potatoes	coupled with the
Saute Sprouts	name of the C.O.
Cauliflower and Bechamel Sauce	Reply by Lt.-Col. W. H. Taylor, D.L.
————	The Permanent Staff Major S. B. Carter, M.B.E.
Hot Sweets	Reply by Capt. H. Woods
Apple Tart and Custard	Our Guests Major H. Davenport Price, M.C.
————	Reply by Superintendent Price
Cold Sweets	The B.B.C. Major H. C. M. Porter, D.S.O.
Fruit Flan	Reply by Percy E. Edgar, Esq.,
Fruit Salad	Mid. Reg. Director
or	
Cheese, Biscuits and Celery	The Entertainers Lieut. F. D. O'Niel
Coffee	Reply by Major H. C. Casey

The Officer's mess dinner menu, 1944.

troops).

I said, 'Right' to my wife, 'we'll be off first thing in the morning', and when it came to the next morning my wife had got the baby all ready, she was just about walking then, got her all ready. I said, 'What are you doing?' She said, 'Well, I'm not going without her', and I said 'Well, I'm not going with her either, because haven't we moved out of London because of the bombing'. Anyway, I went soft because she wouldn't. And when we got to near London, there was an air raid and I kept going. Most vehicles were pulling up, stopping, you know, but I was pushed for time to get to the Drury Lane Theatre and I was going on. Then a policeman came up, stopped me. I said, 'Look, I've got to be at the Drury Lane Theatre at 11.30' I said, 'to audition for entertaining the troops, during the war'. He said, 'Well sir,' he said 'if you'd been on your own, I'd've let you go, but not with a child'. So we had to go in an air raid shelter and we were nearly all day in this ruddy air raid shelter – well, a few hours anyway, and it was too late to go to Drury Lane and we came back home and a week after that I got my calling up papers. That's what they did with artistes – if you were invited to go to an audition and you didn't go, next thing was, I was in the army. I was in there for six and a half years.

Nick Capaldi, born 1913

Driving the Generals

Two of my brothers went into the Grenadier Guards, Bob and David. David went in just before the war and he did six years. Then as soon as he heard the news he got on his bike and caught the next train to London. When he was on the station Sir Francis Davis and Lord Motalman were stood on the station and Sir Francis Davis from Elmley Castle was talking to Lord Montalman from Dumbleton. He said to him, 'Oh this is one of my lads, you know' and our David had just arrived on the train for to go back on duty. Then our Jack had joined the Royal Artillery but they changed from horses to tanks while he was in it. He was at Dunkirk and Alamein. He went through Hell but he never talked about it.

Then Dick went in the Air Force, but he was a mechanic mending planes and doing machinery. They asked him what he'd done before the war and he said he was chauffeur to Dr Wilcox as owned the Lido at Droitwich. He lived in Queen Street, over a shop, he had a flat there and so they said, 'Oh good, if you were a chauffeur to Dr Wilcox you can come and be a chauffeur to the generals!' So Chief Air Marshall, he had to drive all over the different countries to meet Eisenhower, Monty, Churchill, the King, all different ones, you know. During the war he had four Air Chief Marshals to drive for and one was Sir Lessor, one was Garrard and one was Sir Arthur Tedder, Lord Tedder in the finish. He drove him to Tunis to be married to one of the lady officers.

You know whatever car it was and they were up through the mountains and one of these Air Chief Marshals thought Dick was going very slowly once and he says, 'oh, I'll take over' and anyway it was a sheer drop down there, you know what the mountains are in foreign countries, you know like it is in Wales, a sheer drop down the one side and he only did a little way and he said, 'you'd better take over', because he knew that Dick couldn't go any faster!

Catherine Maude Turner, born 1902

Home Guard with Signals Platoon and Women's Auxiliaries.

Signals with the KSLI

I was called up in the war and went to Worcester for my medical. I had no particular trade or anything so they put me in the light infantry: the KSLI. When I went up to Birmingham I had to change at Stonehill station. From Evesham you got to New Street station and I travelled up with the Mayor of Evesham later on. He had a clothes shop in the High Street and he took me, we joined up when we got to Birmingham. He said he'd take me across to Stonehill station but first we'd have a coffee in Lyons Corner House, then he took me on to catch the train back to Stonehill station. When I got to Shrewsbury, where the KSLI was, I got to the main door and as I went in there were some trainees marching on the barrack square and they were going left right, left right and I said 'Good lord, what have I let myself in for?' They were light infantry and they were almost running when

they were marching. They fixed me up with a uniform and other things like shaving kit and whatnot and what they used to called a hussif – I said 'What's this?' They said, 'it's what they call a housewife, a packet of darning needles for your socks and everything for doing temporary repairs'. We had to darn our own socks and things like that. I don't think I was very good at darning. After my initial training, the potential officers and NCOs were put in No. 1 Platoon which is where I went. I volunteered to go on a signals course, for twelve weeks I think it was, and passed as a second year signaller. Then a couple of years later we had a new signals officer who, at that time, didn't know a thing about signalling and he was told to see me. I taught him as much as I could because he had to have a knowledge before he could go into the School of Signals. So I used to spend a little time with him after school telling him what I knew then he passed the signals instructor course with flying colours. He was very grateful to me and he made me an NCO – gave me two stripes. Then it was my turn and I went on a signals instructor course. I did very well, in fact when I got back to the unit, the officer in charge of the school requested that I go back as an instructor. But at that time we were going abroad to the front. Later they found they didn't want us all as a body, but we would be a feeding battalion and when some of the rifle companies were getting depleted we were sent to different places, different battalions. But instead of doing that, the CO at the barracks asked me if I wanted, would I like a job as a signal instructor, so I said 'Oh, yes'. I was very interested at the time. So that's where I went and that's where I was demobbed from – Caterick.

Mr Wilfred John Ayres, born 1916

Royal Army Ordinance Corps

I volunteered when the war broke out in 1939 on my conscience. I think I was about thirty and I volunteered for the army, they grabbed me in and I did the five years. I was in the Royal Army Ordinance Corps, RAOC, and I was a driver for them, taking different units wanting different things, perhaps an ambulance or an ordinary lorry. Our boss'd sort us out: 'I want six men – you, you, you', and I'd take this lorry to the unit and be away three, four days. It might be a long way away and you couldn't travel too far when the war was on. We'd get the rations off the cook, for say, six men. Because I was the lance corporal, I was in charge. I'd say I want six rations for six men for four days and he'd pack it together and away we'd go. We'd stop at night and brew tea, eat what rations he'd give us and make shift like that. We'd deliver the vehicles and then bring old ones back for repair. It was in Italy most of the time.

Harold Robinson, born 1908

Bayoneted Potatoes

We were situated on some market garden land. I was out one day and we'd had an

No. 4 Platoon, 'A' Coy, 4th Worcs Home Guard.

Worcs Home Guard Birthday Parade, Pershore, 1943.

alert and everybody was told to fix bayonets. So we did. And I'm walking in this field and I've got the gun with this bayonet and I just dropped it into the ground, bayonet first, then when I went off and pul'ed it up there was a lovely potato stuck on the end of the bayonet. I went back to the cook and said 'How would you like a nice fresh potato?' 'Oh, go on,' he said. So I put my hand in my pocket and gave it to him. 'My God,' he said, 'Where did you get that?' I said, 'Well, I was walking in that field over there and I dropped my bayonet in the field and it came up with this potato on'. So he says, 'Let's go and have a look'. So we took a ruddy spade and off we went and it was a field of potatoes. We literally must have used that whole field of potatoes eventually.

Nick Capaldi, born 1913

POW in Tripoli

I wasn't at my best then. I'd come out of the RAF, where I'd been a prisoner of war for three years and you know, I mean, skin and thin, I was only just getting my hair back and something, I'd been in hospital for six months with malnutrition. So I wasn't much of a picture to look at, put it that way. I was in North Africa in Libya when the Germans made that big push down towards Alamein, because we got surrounded. There were 2,000 Worcestershire troops captured and Grenadier Guards. We was taken to just outside Tripoli to a makeshift POW camp under a grove of eucalyptus trees and that's where we was for six months. We had dysentery and beri beri, diphtheria. Everything broke out. I got injected and I got fever from it and an abscess from the

Making the oven.

The 8th Worcs' mess tent.

injection. They took me down to hospital to have this thing lanced and while I was down there the British troops landed in Algiers. Course the Italians got a little frightened about that so they shifted all the people out of the hospital to Italy until these gave up and then we went to Germany. We were working in a smelting factory until they couldn't get stuff out of the factory because of the RAF. We finished up an open cast minefield supplying a power station with coal.

We weren't beaten as far that goes. They had these 'brown shirts' I call them, like a home guard in Germany. They carried pistols and everything and although we did have one young kid shot for arguing and things like that, it was more of a mental thing. I used to wake up the morning, stomach churning about what was going to happen today. I was lucky I got back safe, I don't really enjoy really good health now – I've got all the things that old people have.

Bernard Hunt, born 1922

Mr Churchill in My Tank

I tell you the truth, when I was in the army, I was down in Kent by Dover for about a couple of years or so, and people said they got stuff pinched. I never got a thing. I was the only one in the hut with a watch. I bought it from Worcester, on me first leave; it was a square one. In the tank you couldn't wear a watch because of the vibration would shake it to pieces. I used to hang it on a nail in the nissen hut and nobody ever pinched it. No, it was always there. They would say, 'What's the time by Old Joe's watch? It's hanging up there'. Out in the wilds we were. I drove old Churchill down there, he come

down to inspect us and he wandered right round the back of course and my tank was on the end and I was the driver, and the gunner was Harry Norman from Leeds. He says, 'Mr Churchill wants a ride round the battle course' so he got in my tank and I drove him. Harry, a Yorkshire bloke, says, 'Give him some stick, Joe, lad'. He was all right! He had his hard hat on, his cigar in his mouth, well he looked a bit white, he congratulated us on a nice run, because he went down these big holes with this tank and up the other side and bang! We shook him up a bit, but he congratulated us when he come out. I joined up in '42, that was about '43, before the invasion, when we moved, sailed from Gosport to Normandy, you see.

Joe Sherwood, born 1923

Flame Throwing Tanks

Then, after the war, I was still a young bloke and they was going to transfer me to Japan and the flame throwing tanks, for the main invasion of Japan. But the old colonel said to us, he says, 'Don't you get taken prisoner, you lads – they'll have no mercy on you blokes'. My brother was out there see, a regular soldier. But then they dropped the atom bomb and stopped that. Till then, we had to go in the Regular Army. I went into the Hussars then, one of these Irish spit and polish cavalry regiments. We was stationed in Berlin. I was one of the guards at Pottsdam, saluted to Montgomery. I got a picture at home of the Victory Parade in Berlin, when they come in. It was made into a Christmas card. I've still got it in the drawer at home. And there's Churchill, Montgomery and all the rest, and I'm up at

14th Platoon, 'C' Company, taken after six weeks initial training, Bodmin, Cornwall. Joe Sherwood is second from the left in the middle row.

'B' Squadron, 147th Regiment, Royal Armoured Corps, Holland 1944, just after Ardens. Joe Sherwood is in the top left corner.

Victory Parade in Berlin, 21 July 1945.

the top there: 1945 that was: July 5 1945, Victory Parade in Berlin.

Joe Sherwood, born 1923

Painting Jerry Tanks

On the victory march in Berlin they made the Jerrys paint all the tanks. The Brits, they had to wear pumps so as not to scratch the paint. Once the tanks were lined up they swapped the pumps for their best boots and the Jerrys had to go along the ranks and dust the boots.

Joe Sherwood, born 1923

Rationing At Home

Yanks to Stay

During the war I had folks from all over England to stay with me, two weeks here and there. I had them from London, Birmingham and Hendon and over the other side of Malvern Hills and American medical officers I had too, one from Massachusetts and one from Nevada. Raymond Lapse came from Massachusetts, he said they'd been on a route march and Fred said, 'Where did you go on your route march, round the square? Oh gosh, you don't call that a route march – we was there for a walk on Sunday afternoon, that's no route march!' Then we had Jerry Green, he came from Nevada. He was a farmer's son and he went out the day the invasion was when all the country roads was absolutely packed with vehicles for going forward. There was bits of guns, all the side roads and everything was loaded with stuff to be moved gradually forward. They could never understand when they stayed with me, these medical officers, why they had to put up a great marquee in the Crown Meadow, put all the medical stuff out, pack it all up, take the tent down, next day put it all up again, unpack it all, day after day, day after day they had to do that. When they got out there after 4 July, they were following Patton's army and they had to keep on putting their tents up and the medical stuff and they

were getting the wounded from the front and passing them on back there. I had a letter from Jerry Green to show me how many bandages they used every night, for all these wounded.

Catherine Maude Turner, born 1902

Getting Rid of the Gasmasks

I've still got my gas mask. We had to carry these on our backs, wherever we went. It doesn't matter if we had a pretty dress on; we still had to stick this ugly thing on. The thing's still there, its heavy. We had to carry that on our backs, but only for a year because they said if we can see a way which you don't have to carry it, we will get rid of it and as time went on there was

'B' Squadron, 147th Regiment, Royal Armoured Corps, Holland 1944, with a Churchill Tank. Joe Sherwood is in the top left corner.

no talk of a gas attack. This was the Second World War. They gave it out on the wireless that there was no further need to wear your gas mask. And it was no joke, especially if you were dressed up. I must take care of that. It was in the newspapers and all – as soon we're safe and we think we can do without them, we'll not waste another hour. And then the time came when they said there was no talk of gas attacks, there wasn't one at all, right up to the end, that was one thing they didn't do, only at the front line.

Ethel Marion Heritage, born 1913

Sleeping at Longbridge

Longbridge was called the Austin Motor Works and I lived in a house there. Every night we had to be down in a shelter underground, after we'd done a day's work. That was your bed. Not very nice, not after you'd done a day's work to have to go to bed down underground but there were always there because of the motor works and there were big balloons up above, they were full of gas. If they shot at them they could injure people.

Ethel Marion Heritage, born 1913

Spy Balloon

I took a photograph of a balloon, but that's nothing to do with the war. That was reconnaissance, spying for the war. They were Germans in that one out to spy on us; this was a few years before the war in 1932.

Ethel Marion Heritage, born 1913

'Put That Light Out!'

There were five of us, I've got a sister down the road here, three brothers, there were five of us. One took up gardening, the others went in other jobs. Two of them went in the war, one was a sailor, one was a soldier and the other one stayed at home and they wouldn't release him because he'd got land. It wasn't very quiet – people shouting out 'put that light out' all the time. That's how it was. You had to see there were no cracks in the curtains, a shade over your bicycle lamp, don't wear black at night, wear white, wear something white at night so you could be seen because of the blackout. I rode to Evesham on my bike one day with a friend of mine; I had an acetylene lamp. A great big lamp on the front with these little gritty things in – put me in mind of grit. And it caught fire, I was along Waterside and it caught fire, somebody shouted out 'Put that light out!' and I said, 'I can't!' 'I tell you, put that bloody light out'. I started to cry – it was beyond me, until the stuff had all gone. Don't ask me how I got home because I can't remember, but I did. There was a raid on as well. They didn't bomb Evesham, they were looking for Redditch where the firearms were – BSA.

Ethel Marion Heritage, born 1913

Celebrations in Warden Street

I can remember standing with my mother on this balcony and watching the people flowing down Warden Street and half of them were well oiled, singing the war was over – that the First World War was over.

Barbara Harris, born 1914

The Home Guard at Elmley Castle with Lt Russell (left) and CSM Allcock (right).

Sgt Harris' Wife

You'd be surprised what they dropped in that First World War – quite heavy stuff. The houses rocked and mother grabbed me in her arms and down into the basement and stayed there for a time. And then later on in that war she didn't feel altogether safe in that house. I was wrapped in a shawl and had a little stripey hat put on my head and I was carried out to the police station. Mother went up the steps with this in her arms and said to the policeman on duty, 'Sgt Harris?' And he said, 'Sgt Harris has already gone in, you'll have to wait down there'. She said, 'I'm Sgt Harris' legal wife and this is his child. I cannot go down those stairs and into that basement with this child'. And so he let her in and we went in to where they were and I think it was perhaps the police mess room, quite a long room and there were tables put up – two huge tables. One policeman stood at one end and those people sang *Pack up your Troubles in your Old*

Above: *The Allies, 1915.*

Below: *Soldiers in Evesham, 1942.*

Peace Celebrations – Children's day.

Kit Bag and those people at the other end sang, *It's a Long Way to Tipperary* and they did it together to make a noise to drown what was going on outside – I didn't understand what was going on at that time

Barbara Harris (in London), born 1914

German POWs Living Next Door

I was born at Hinton on the Green, the crossroads going to Cheltenham. There's a house at the side of the crossroads on the left, I was born in that house. I was there for three years then I moved up the lane towards Childswick, and there's a house up that lane, next up the Cheltenham road, like that. I lived up there, this was the First World War, and we had German prisoners of war living next door. They were captured and put in that house because it was empty. They did that in wartime, you don't know do you? It was a derelict house, empty. They bunged them in there. We couldn't understand them but they were civil – they had to be I expect. I was only three then and then they moved on to Banbury from there. By Banbury Cross – ride a cock horse.

Ethel Marion Heritage, born 1913

Coming Home

Best Gunner

My husband was moved to a place called Tonbridge, then all over Kent, then to Wimbledon. They called it Merton then.

The next thing was Greenoch in Scotland, then he was overseas. He sailed for Singapore but when he was in Cape Town, refuelling, Singapore fell. So then they were re-routed to the Middle East. He was at El Alamein and he was shot in the hand. The Lieutenant said, 'I don't want you to go sick. You're my best gunner'. He said, 'But I can't stand the pain', so he went to the MO and he said, 'You'll have to let him go, see that red line? If you don't, he'll be dead by morning. That's blood poisoning'. When he was in hospital he met a man he went to school with. He said, 'Hey 'Greeny', there's a job coming up that'll suit you. It's looking after prisoners of war'. They say in the British Army, 'Never volunteer for anything' – so he did! They looked after Germans in one camp – and Italians in another. They didn't want to escape. We had five leaves together then

he was gone. The last time I saw him I went to London on the train. When I went back in the carriage I said to a woman, 'That's the last I'll see of him for a time. He's had his embarkation leave'.

Doris Greenhalf, born 1913

Oh, Bad Egg!

Well, after three and a half years they said he could come back. I said, 'Stay where you are, the second front's coming'. He had a good job and I was getting money and banking every penny of it. He came from Port Suez over the Mediterranean. The storms were terrible and they had to put into Malta for three days. Even the sailors were sick. Then he came from the toe of Italy right up by train. I knew he was on his

Peace Day at Hampton, 1919.

way because his letters stopped. He came into Newhaven. That was on a Friday night. We had no cars in those days, there weren't any so I took his bike to meet him at Evesham station, and I met two trains. He wasn't on them. I though, 'Oh, bad egg! There's one more train from Paddington. I'll meet that'. Well, he bowled out. He was that dirty I couldn't see him. I said, 'The first thing you want is a bath'. He said, 'I want a bath and a good sleep'.

Doris Greenhalf, born 1913

Into Civvies

When we got home – it was just as usual, they gave us civilian clothes, a suit and a hat.

Harold Robinson, born 1908

Never Away From Home Again

When Jack came back from Dunkirk and Alamein he married and lived at Lenchwick. He built his own bungalow and he had a paddock and put in floral trees and heather. He had a lovely place there but he never wanted to go on holiday or anything. They went to go on holiday once and he got a Labrador dog and they put the dog in kennels and they only stayed away a weekend and back they came and fetched the dog and he said I don't want to go away from home again. He never wanted to go again.

Catherine Maude Turner, born 1902

The Tank in Abbey Park, c. 1920.

Joe Sherwood and his nephew Oliver revisit a Churchill Tank at the Tank museum Bodminton, Dorset.

CHAPTER 7

High Days and Holidays

The World Fair, 1912.

Left the Potatoes On

We went to see the Robins at Crystal Palace. We went to Ascot as well with the British Legion because I worked for the British Legion for forty-six years. I got a certificate there and a royal brooch at the back of the clock. Oh, we had a lovely time there but we lost. We had a lovely time. We went by train in those days, by train. Years later, when my house got broke into, Benny Stokes was broken into the same day as mine.

Benny Stokes was a footballer and he got drunk that day, so they got him in a wheelbarrow and wheeled him along the station and they put him in a train and sent him home before we went, because he was, I don't know why he got drunk, because we lost, I'm sure.

Anyway, I'll tell you what, we used to go to Ascot with the British Legion, all of us from the British Legion and we picked up other folks as well, village people, and this one time we were going up the Cotswolds one day and a woman got up and said, 'Driver, STOP!' She said, 'at the next telephone, anywhere you see a telephone, you stop'. So there was a telephone at the side of the road somewhere we went and her and another woman got out and went to this telephone, we didn't know what was happening. Anyway, when we got to Henley on Thames we went and had our coffee and Edna ordered the dinner for the night for coming back and when we were loaded up ready to go onto Ascot, a police sergeant stood on the doorstep of the bus and he said. 'Is the lady here who came into our station just now and rung up for the gas to be turned off, her gas stove with potatoes on?' and we all burst out laughing. It turned out that this Mrs … from Hampton had put the potatoes on while she was getting ready to go and she'd forgot them and left them on.

Catherine Maude Turner, born 1902

Cooeed the Queen

Oh, well course we used to go, we used to love to see the fancy hats [at Ascot]. There was that Mrs Simpkins, she always had, whatever her name was, gorgeous looking hats and then there was one all feathers as used to do betting and Fred said keep away from him he may be lousy because he was a dirty old man. He was all feathers he seemed to me, but we used to go on the poor side, not the rich side where the queen was. Anyway you'll be interested to know this, the queen and the royal party were coming up the course in the carriages, to go onto the big stand, the royal stand, and there was a lady behind me with a camera and a great big policeman in front of me and we crowded all to see the royal family come down. This lady said, 'Oh dear, she's looking the other way', so I said 'Cooee' at the top of my voice and the queen looked this way and she said, 'Thank you', and the queen looked across and waved. The policeman never said anything and this lady was ever so grateful. I think she come from Canada from how she spoke, she was so pleased that the queen had looked this way. So I said I've cooeed the queen.

Catherine Maude Turner, born 1902

Holidays

Plum Picking at Holiday Time

When we had the children little and he had holidays, we used to have a few days plum picking, then we'd go out for the day, take the kiddies out for a treat, that's how we used to do it – we never had holidays.

Florence Edna Elizabeth Hunt, born 1927

Weston for the Day

Well, we had holidays, I used to try and work it that we had a week plum picking and got some money together plum picking and the kids did, then we'd say lets got down to Weston for the day and spend it.

Bernard Hunt, born 1922

Easter

Climbing Evesham Tower

On Ascension Day, you were supposed to climb up Evesham tower, all over the Vale you could see. I went up once, that's all. The Regatta was on and it was a bit flooded, I went up to the top and had a look.

Fred Williams, born 1912 in conversation with May Williams, born 1916

Eggs For Easter

At Easter we only had ordinary chicken's eggs. We never saw a chocolate egg when we were little. On Easter morning my mother would put on a saucepan, there were five of us and she'd put in about a dozen eggs. And that was treat. We could have as many eggs as we liked. You were all trying to beat one another. We didn't do a lot with them, because if you had bread and butter you couldn't eat a lot of the eggs, could you?!

Kate Spilsbury, born 1911

Dyeing Eggs

They were all coloured; you put them in coloured water. You'd use cochineal or another dye.

Sylvia Hickenbothan, born 1913

Mayday

We used to gather bunches of cowslips and pull out the little flower and you've got the honey at the bottom, lovely. Every first of May, well the day before, my mother used to send us out to pick cowslips and they had to go on the mat outside the back door,

scatter a few, and outside the front door. Anyone who came in, brought you good luck and if you had visitors and they went out you brought them good luck if you had cowslips on your mats.

Honor Clements, born 1915

Blossom Sunday

We always brought my mother and father round Evesham in the blossom time because it's a sight! My mother wasn't satisfied unless she'd seen the blossom when it was out. Blossom Sunday was a regularized thing. When they can see the blossom coming out they classify it as Blossom Sunday. The tourists come round the route to see the blossom. You go along the country roads and see the signs up, apple blossom route or plum blossom route. It would usually be May. You'd go round and see the blossom and then we'd end up having gales and blow it off!

Honor Clements, born 1915 in conversation with Betty Jones, born 1910

Halloween

We would always have a party on Halloween at night and that was considered my birthday treat, so I always thought I was born on the 31, until I got my birth certificate, which wasn't so many years ago. So now I know it I was born 30 October 1911. It was a party for the children round about and we always had a big bathtub of water and apples and have to try and get these apples out the water. With your hands tied behind your back and a sometimes a blindfold. It'd be going round and round, trying to get a bite out of it. They weren't always sweet apples either!

Kate Spilsbury, born 1911

Christmas

Weighing for Christmas

You could safely say that a couple of months before Christmas you would never get out of the shop before eight or nine o'clock at night because everything had to be weighed up for the next day – butter, lard, margarine, sugar – it used to come in big sacks of sugar and you'd have three of you -- one would fill the bags of sugar temporarily, the one next going along would weigh it and the one of the end would seal it down. As I say, that took most of the day. Tea came in packets, that was the only thing that did come ready packed.

Wilfred John Ayres, born 1916

Christmas at Gran's

My Gran started two or three weeks before Christmas, cooking. I mean, she made all her own puddings in the coal boiler, the furnace. And she used to do all her own mincemeat, she used to make all her own Christmas pudding, mince pies. She made everything. She wouldn't buy anything. Sometimes she'd have give her a whole ham which she used to hang up a few weeks before Christmas, because they reckoned it tasted better if you hung 'em up. She used to do these whole hams and then she had this

suckling pig in the middle of the table. She used to do all her own pickled onions. She started weeks before Christmas; it took her weeks. And she had everything – you mention it, it was there and she used to do it all herself. She only had a small house – a three-bedroomed house – well it was called three bedroomed, one was a little cubbyhole really, you could barely get a bed in there. It was bigger than my mum's but it was still small really, for her family, but you could say there was a good twenty I should think round that table for her dinner, with her daughters and husbands and family. I mean, sometimes us kids had to wait till after because they couldn't get us all round. There was always plenty left anyway. And then after that, after everything was done, dinner was over, a cup of tea made all round, although there was drink on the table, there was always beer on the table.

In the evening was music night. Everybody had the party piece and every year they always done the same party piece. Mother on the piano, I had two uncles and they used to dress up at Christmas as a couple of minstrels. They used to black their faces, one had a ukulele and one had a banjo, you think they'd sound the same, but they don't, they sound different. They blacked their face and had a straw hat. They'd go to the pub and have a drink and then on Christmas Eve, there used to be all of us, go to a little pub around the corner – it's still there today, the Dugout, and my Gran used to live just the next street round. Christmas Eve, they'd start at this pub, have a couple or three drinks, play this music and then they'd go out and everybody used to follow them and they'd go out and up along High Street, playing this music and the folks walking along behind, out of the pub. Then they'd go down Bridge Street, then into the

Market Place, then back down to Gran's. By the time they'd finished there used to be rows of people behind them. They wouldn't be allowed to do it today would they, the police wouldn't allow it, it'd be disturbing the peace. The police used to join in anyway.

Dorothy May Sollis, born 1921

Letter Upside Down

When I was six we went to the juniors and we had to learn double writing. I can remember writing this letter to Father Christmas because he was supposed to be coming that night. Anyway, when we went in the morning, there was nothing there, 'Oh he hasn't been', I thought. But on this blackboard where I'd pinned my note, what I'd like, it said, 'You left your letter upside down so I haven't left anything'. I was sure I'd pinned it up the right way, but that's what Father Christmas wrote on this blackboard.

Lottie Buckingham, born 1923

New Year

First-footing

Until recent years, I was terribly superstitious, because my husband was ash blond and I wouldn't let him out. They never used to let anyone, but a dark man in on the first of the year. Until I left Tewkesbury, the man who lived opposite me was very dark and although they didn't believe in it, he always came across just after midnight. And he used to carry a piece of coal, a slice of bread: bread signifying you wouldn't want through the

year, coal so you'd have enough fuel. The coal was put in the fire and the bread was placed on the table.

They would come in through, usually the front door. They'd walk round the table in the lounge into the living room round the table there and then out and they'd go down to the gate at the bottom of the yard and they'd open that and come back and sit down and have a glass of wine and a mince pie.

My first son was very dark. He used to get up at five on New Year's day and go all the way round. If it's youngsters like that you used to give them a shilling. Roger used to get half a crown if he did five houses.

My mother was really upset one year– I let the cat out just before midnight and of course somebody opened the door to come in and the cat came in first. Oh my mother was furious! She swore the bad luck we had the following year was all due to the fact the cat came in.

Honor Clements, born 1915

Bringing a Piece of Coal

We had parties. They came in with a piece of coal and they didn't go out, until they went home. If they went out they'd take the luck with them.

Betty Jones, born 1910

Fairs and Carnivals

The Evesham Mop

When they had the mop, once a year, a big fair, that was all the way High Street. We used

Morris Dancers at Old English Fair, 1909.

to save up for that, when the Mop came in October, having rides on the horses and that. I remember on Sunday they used to have a little service and you know the horses that go round and round – they had one of these big organ things and they used to play the hymns on that. I suppose I'd be in my teens then.

Phyllis Reay, born 1914

The Carnival

We used to have Carnivals here that went for the week. We used to go all round the villages, we went to a different village every night collecting and it was always for the hospital. The Gala procession was on the Saturday and all the firms decorated their own vans and lorries. They came from everywhere. Not only Evesham did it locally, but all round Evesham and Worcester. We had it for about twenty years, when Chubby Mason, the manager of the bank was Carnival King for years – a big fat portly man, manager of Barclays Bank and he was always Carnival King and all the young pretty girls as Carnival Queen. And they used to have jesters. Everybody joined in. We did the work, the catering for it. My son was always in it; he was a jester in it, near the Queen. It must be fifty years ago he did that. We used to enjoy the days going around the villages because they made us all welcome. And we made such a lot of money.

Betty Jones, born 1910

Swimming Gala

The swimming club used to have a swimming Gala and we had swimming in the water and greasy poles, tug of war – one crew one side of the river and the other crew

Evesham Carnival, c. 1940.

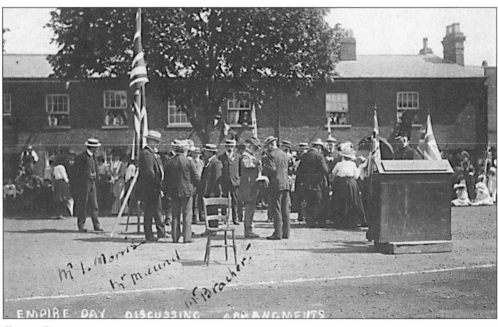

Empire Day arrangements.

The Old English Fair, 1909.

the other side, until one crew managed to pull the other into the water. But it was all in good fun and they were dressed for it you know. But eventually as the swimmers got older there weren't the young ones coming up. There were other things to do which seemed more interesting and weren't so hard.

Betty Jones, born 1910

CHAPTER 8

How It Was

Bridge Street, c. 1900.

Sawmills on Blackberry Edge

Years ago there used to be the sawmills, along on the Blackberry Edge, down that side, before you get to the Worcester Road. Up the street the horses used to bring elm trees chained, about three trunks of trees, and it took about three or four horses to pull them up Bridge Street. We used to see them because they'd anchor another horse on to come up Bridge Street because it was so heavy, and they used to take them to the sawmills. That was all done for building, all the trees. Then there was three or four butchers, and a fishmongers in Bridge Street. That's all gone, you know. In High

Street there was a pork butchers and Collins'.

Catherine Maude Turner, born 1902

Lived in a Manor House

Well first of all we went to live at Sedgeberrow on the Cheltenham Road. There weren't any buses or anything like that so we all used to have to have bicycles. I was fine, I loved it, but my poor mother never took to it, she was always falling off. We lived in what had originally been a manor house, not very big, but very, very old. It belonged to a farmer and he made it into two and my mum and dad had the one half. We stayed there for about three years and then we came into Evesham and it was very, very different to what it is now. Quiet, you know, but all sorts of things – they used to bring all the cattle and all the things into market though the town.

Phyllis Reay, born 1914

Strawsons, the Drapers

I used to work for Mr Abbot who took over Strawsons, the drapers in Bridge Street. They used to hang all sorts of clothes outside to show things off, the window was a display and when you went in it was all hangers and things like that, fixtures with towels and material, it was all fixtures. When you took the money you used to have those pulleys. You took the money, put it in the cup, screwed it up, pulled the cord and it shot off to the office and they sent it back with the change. They had that in Strawsons and also in George Masons, the grocer's in Bridge Street.

May Williams, born 1916

Espley Saw Mills.

Market Opposite the Station

I think the market was every week and it used to be opposite the station, it's houses now and Bridge Street is very different; it used to be all lovely little cottages, you went down steps to them; that's all gone. They used to have big markets as well, right in the High Street for vegetables and the like. It's a great area, or it was, for growing asparagus and the plums. They used to have all the High Street full of big chips as they called them, the big baskets, big hamper things.

Phyllis Reay, born 1914

Shopping at Woolworths

Well of course, most of the shopping was done in Woolworths, because there was nothing over sixpence in Woolworths. You could buy shoes, pumps, stockings, well, everything, you name it you could buy it.

Dorothy Sollis, born 1921

The Round House

The Round House is called the Round House because you can walk all round it!

Doris Greenhalf, born 1913

Evesham's Changed

That ornamental entrance to where the park is now there used to be some cottages and they used to be in a dip and there were iron bars along the top. When we were kids we used to swing round them and the old

The Round House.

The Mayor and Corporation.

lady used to sell fishing tackle and bait. Now they've changed it all again.

Doris Greenhalf, born 1913

A Relation's House

We had a house; a relation of ours had a house at Broadway, I can't remember the name of it now, it's by the old yard and a relation of ours used to drive the coaching horses from London to Worcester. He was the coach driver and they lived at this big house, an antique place now, ever such a lot of windows, I can't remember the name of it now. I keep on thinking of Dresden House, but that's where Aunt Min came to school in Evesham up the High Street with railings round. It's some house, next to yew tree, bell

yard. There's a yard up Broadway on the left as you go up and the stables were up there. All those stables have been made into cottages now in Broadway and the silver was stolen from there one night and I gave matron one of the last things with a 'D' on it.

Catherine Maude Turner, born 1902

Ill Abed

Mother's uncle was the postmaster of Broadway when it was next to the Fosses, the chemist. I was looking up this passage one day; they used to live behind the post office. I've got a letter, he wrote to uncle Charlie from there, at the back of the post office, 'ill abed' he called it – he wrote it to his sister at the Walnuts, he thanked her very much for sending the oysters and a drop of the 'hard stuff'! He was much better for the 'hard stuff' it said. Uncle Arthur was born there in 1800 and mother was the last one, she was the youngest, and she was born in 1878 and she lived till she was sixty and died in 1930 something – before the war in any case. Our Bob died when he was twenty-two in the Grenadier Guards and that killed her really.

Catherine Maude Turner, born 1902

The Bells

I lived over on Merstow Green – I had my daughter, she was seven and I know I took her into the churchyard to see this business. The bells from the bell tower were recast you see, they put more bells in the bell tower to make the carillon more tunes, they were very limited. They made them up to fourteen, they were seven before, went over the same seven each week. Well it made it a fortnight then. They played every three hours – nine o'clock was the start in the morning, not in the night, nine, twelve, three, six and nine, not midnight. Five times and then there was a hymn on each of the two Sundays. There were fourteen altogether, there were only seven till this was done but they built it up to fourteen. My father remembered the bells being played. He used to talk about it when I was a little girl and I'm eight-seven now, so that's a long

The bell tower.

time ago. They played tunes like the *Eaton Boating Song*, *Drink to Me Only with Thine Eyes*, *Come Lasses and Lads* and the *Bluebells of Scotland*. They're going to try and make even more tunes to go over a longer period you see. I used to love to go in the park and listen to them. When I was young I used to do my shopping and take it down the park. I was never in a hurry because I got home quicker than I do now. It's as much as I can do now to do it and get back, but I used to go in the park after and take it with me and sit and listen to these tunes. I knew them all by heart. Then there's the silver bells, that's the carillon. There's quite a bit about the carillon. They promised this by the end of the year now. They keep putting it off because they can't get the money. £15,000 they want. Well I give a bit now and then, but we can't give that much, can we? I send a bit to the church now and then, shows I'm willing because my father used to talk about it. Then there was the silver bells – there are some silver bells hidden somewhere in Evesham.

Ethel Marion Heritage, born 1913

High and Low Church

We have two churches here in the same churchyard. I used to go to St Lawrence, which was the low church, but now they don't use it for services so I've had to go over to All Saints, which was very high at one time.

The low church was a much more plain service, we didn't go in for lots of candles and bowing and what have you. But years ago it was meant for the poor people and the people that were coming through, walking, they could have a meal there – I'm going

The Bell.

back donkey's years now. But the high church was for the posh folks. But now, it's a nice church, but I preferred the old one.

Phyllis Reay, born 1914

Elizabethan Mural

You know the place which says Journal. That's a very historical building. I worked there. We had a shop down below. It had been a shop since the 1800 and something and it was a modest, rather old fashioned Victorian shop and the two ladies who started it, by the name of Trinder, they moved away to Worcester. It was taken on by the two senior assistants, by the name of Hughes, two maiden ladies, Miss Ethel Hughes and Miss Winnie Hughes and it went on quietly and modestly and began to be increasingly favoured by certain

Gun Week, 1918.

customers. I helped to build up the trade to a great extent. The premises were historic and it went downstairs, right down underneath a winding stone stair slabs staircase with no hand rail of course. We made our way carefully down till we got to the cellar. The cellar floor was composed of tiny pieces of stone stamped into the earth, about an inch wide; they were called setts, I think and I know I felt there was something about the building, I thought this must have been here for many, many years.

Later on we were having operations done upstairs. There were two rooms looking out onto the High Street and we thought it would be a good idea to do away with that division, wood and plaster, division and make it into one long room. I went up, nosy

me, to see how the men were getting on with their work and of course there was plaster and dust and everything. And one of the men said – over on that wall, there's some sort of writing, 'Oh really, what is it, I wonder', so I went under this archway through. You know what it was? – an Elizabethan wall mural. You know how Queen Elizabeth I was dressed? There was a lady and a gentleman and in the centre was a Tudor rose in every other square. I thought this is interesting – there must be something about this, so I went back downstairs to my employers and I said you know, there's some sort of writing up there, I think we ought to find out about it. So we had a Mr Kenneth Gil Smith come in and he belonged to the Smiths Journal, original firm. And he said, 'Yes – I believe this could be genuine Elizabethan'. They thought it was originally an inn. I think the building was one of the oldest building in the High Street. I think the cradle of Evesham was just about there.

Barbara Harris, born 1914

Otter Hunting

In those days they used to have otter hunting. We used to have days off from school to go otter hunting – which I wouldn't do now, I think its horrible. It was just a day out then. I never saw them kill one.

Phyllis Reay, born 1914

The Duc d'Orleans

The Duc d'Orleans was pretender to the throne of France you see. When Wood Norton was in his hands, a 14ft fence, wire fence all the way round the estate, right through Lenchwick and up along Worcester Road and then you pass the Golden Gates when you go along there. He used to keep bears and wolves. There was bearpits there. Then it was a boys' school and then, during the war, the BBC was there and they used to broadcast from there, Sandy McPherson used to play the organ and then it got struck over the front door, by a bomb. Fred said that nothing ever touched that organ because they got it sandbagged up so much that it didn't do any damage at all.

Catherine Maude Turner, born 1902

Wood Norton Hall, 1904.

The Shooting Party at Wood Norton Hall, 1904.

The Ducd'Orlean's shooting party at Wood Norton Hall with game laid out, 1904.

Chasses du 28 et 29 Novembre 1904

ont pris part

La Majesté	Le Roi de Portugal
Monseigneur	Le Duc d'Orléans
S.A.R.M^r.	Le Duc de Guise
Monsieur	Le Duc de Luynes
,,	Le Colonel Legge
,,	E. Aubry-Vitet
,,	Le Baron de Fonscolombe
,,	G. de Monicourt

The guests at the shooting party.

Battues : Norton, Hipton Hills, Wood Norton Park

Dates	28	29	Contre-pied	Totaux
Faisans	1570	1919	76	3565
Perdrix	4			4
Lièvres	22			22
Lapins	116	816	50	982
Canards Sauvages		41		41
Pigeons ramiers		9	4	13
Divers	17	25		42
Totaux, par jour	1729	2810	130	

Total Général   4669

1 cerf tué par Sa Majesté le Roi de Portugal

The bag of the shooting party.

Fireworks at Wood Norton Hall, 1904.

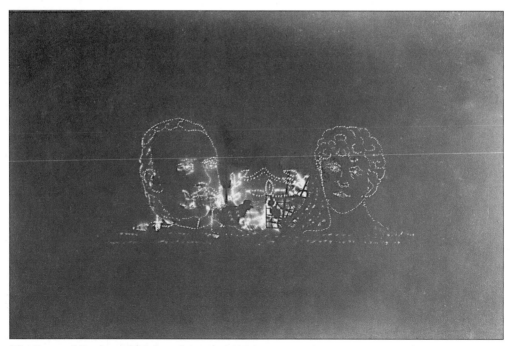

The Duc and Duchesse D'Orlean fireworks, 1904.

Badsey Pike

As you go down Badsey Pike, its called British Legion now, that was what we called the Old School. The British Legion took it over. All round there were orchards of different fruit and things so we had all that to play on. You could go down Monks; that's between the Manor and another house. If you walk down Monks this man used to farm mink for fur. Then you'd come out into Badsey Lane and there was a big barn and two black and white cottages there. A lot of it's built on now. Then there was the Vicarage. That was really spooky because it had big tall trees.

Sandra Grady, born 1943

Room Where Prince Edward Died

They used to use this one room for storage, for paper bags and also the toilet was up there, they had a curtain across and then a corridor and you had to go down this little passage to get to it. I was going down this little passage one day, I moved the paper bags and there was this big mark, almost like fresh blood, slightly brown, and it was right across the room. I went down to the boss, and said, 'There's a brown mark up there'. 'Oh lass', he called me lass, because my mother's name was Honor and they used to get mixed, 'Oh lass, I wish you hadn't asked me that, you won't want to go up there any more'. I said: 'Why?' He said, 'That's the room that Prince Edward died in and all the scrubbing in the world isn't able to move it!' He and his wife, they lived there and he's supposed to walk on the 1st May because he died on the 2nd. Well, I never saw him, but I used to dread going down there.

Sometimes, before I got there, you could see the curtain move and it would even go along the pole, just as thought someone pulling it. I stayed there a year. They've torn it down now, but the panelling was fantastic, real oak, all in squares. You couldn't see a handle, but every so often you could just press, I knew where then and it would slide and there was a little tiny cupboard where you could keep money, because they all kept it at home those days; all these little secret cupboards.

Honor Clements, born 1915

Haunted Home

It was a lovely house, where we lived. Apparently, years and years before we went there, it used to have a moat. There was still a part of it when we went there, my dad used to keep ducks in it! There was a little room; one bigger room – a living room come kitchen with a big range, a fire to cook with and then there was a huge pantry! Big stone slab, very, very high with all sorts of shelves. There was a lovely staircase in our half, very wide treads with a lovely banister that went up so far and a gallery at the top. That was a big room with a window and a window seat which I thought was lovely. Then there was one tiny little room, a box room; then a middle size room, which my parents had, and then a one big room, but although it was upstairs, half of it was stone floor! And the other half was very wide black oak, so my mother just had rugs over it. The window had bars over it. It was sash window, but when you opened it, it vanished, the bit went straight down into the windowsill and I had this big room all to myself. It was supposed to be haunted. It never bothered me – I never saw anything. But I had an aunt who came to stay once and they told her about this. Now because this was such a big room, my mother had odd bits of furniture up there and there was a settee up there and there was a little closet I suppose. Now the settee was in front of the closet, we didn't really use it, just kept things in it. Well, when my aunt came she slept with me and she woke up in the middle of the night and said she thought she heard something. In the morning the settee was right away from the closet and the door was open. It had never happened before, but she always swore it was a ghost. It was mentioned in one of the history books. King Charles came this way and they reckoned he spent a night there, on his way to Warwick. But the girls in the village used to talk. They all reckoned

it was haunted. There was one girl I was friendly with; my mum and dad were going out one night to a dance. In those days it was quite something to go out late at night like that. Anyway, they said someone could come round and sleep with me. So this girl said she'd like to come and we tried to keep awake all night to see the ghost. We never saw anything, but she was quite chuffed to think she's spent the night there.

Phyllis Reay, born 1914

Like Going on Holiday

They used to laugh at me when I was a child. My aunt died and I was downstairs by myself and my mother was upstairs. She came downstairs and I said, 'Mum, I've just seen auntie Fibi'. She said, 'Don't be daft, child, she's dead'. I said, 'I know, but she was sitting in Dad's chair and she nodded and smiled at me'. I mean, I didn't know, I don't think I was old enough to realize that they called them ghosts or anything. So my mother always said I was fey. When you're a child you don't understand death. But when you get old you lose all fear of it. It's like going on a holiday except you don't need to pack a case.

Honor Clements, born 1915

The Woolpack, Port Street, in the 1920s.